THE TRAGICAL HISTORY OF
DOCTOR FAUSTUS

Christopher Marlowe

PRESTWICK HOUSE
LITERARY TOUCHSTONE CLASSICS™

P.O. BOX 658 • CLAYTON, DELAWARE 19938

Senior Editor: Paul Moliken

Editor: Darlene Gilmore

Cover Design: Chris Koniencki

Production: Jeremy Clark

Prestwick House
Literary Touchstone Classics

P.O. Box 658 • Clayton, Delaware 19938
Tel: 1.800.932.4593
Fax: 1.888.718.9333
Web: www.prestwickhouse.com

Prestwick House Teaching Units™, Activity Packs™, and Response Journals™ are the perfect complement for these editions. To purchase teaching resources for this book, visit www.prestwickhouse.com/material

This Prestwick House edition is an unabridged republication with slight emendations of *The Tragical History of Doctor Faustus*, published in 1909, by Sturgis & Walton Co., New York.

ISBN 978-1-58049-798-5

CONTENTS

NOTES

What is a literary classic and why are these classic works important to the world?

A literary classic is a work of the highest excellence that has something important to say about life and/or the human condition and says it with great artistry. A classic, through its enduring presence, has withstood the test of time and is not bound by time, place, or customs. It speaks to us today as forcefully as it spoke to people one hundred or more years ago, and as forcefully as it will speak to people of future generations. For this reason, a classic is said to have universality.

Christopher Marlowe was born in Canterbury, England, on February 6, 1564, the son of a shoemaker. He was educated at King's College and Corpus Christi College and received a Master's degree in 1587. This award was not based solely on scholarship, however, and Marlowe's life of political machinations and possible spying for the English government began around the same time that he received it. Queen Elizabeth's Privy Council awarded the degree, stating that "he had done Her Majesty good service, & deserved to be rewarded for his faithful dealing in matters touching the benefit of the country." Much of what Marlowe did politically in his life remains unknown, another fact that leads many to conclude that he played a part in secretive government activities.

He became friendly with both Sir Phillip Sidney and Sir Walter Raleigh. Influenced by them and determined to become one of the English literati, Marlowe wrote his first play, *Tamburlaine the Great,* which was performed as early as 1587, but not published until 1590. The play is one of the first ever written in blank verse, and it elevated that poetic form to high art. He continued his writing career, producing such works as *The Jew of Malta* (1589-1590), *Edward II* (1593), and *The Tragical History of Dr. Faustus* (1604).

However, just two years after the publication of *Tamburlaine the Great,* Marlowe was imprisoned for participating in a fatal swordfight that took the life of an innkeeper's son; Marlowe spent just two weeks in jail and was found not guilty of murder.

The Tragical History of Dr. Faustus, Marlowe's masterpiece, was first performed in 1588, but did not appear in the official records until later. Within this same time period, Marlowe was arrested for counterfeiting, but was released with no reason given, which lends additional credence to the spying-for-the-Crown theory. Some scholars speculate that Marlowe was also working as a double agent, which would have made his already risky life extremely dangerous.

In 1592, the Queen's Privy Council closed the theaters because of their portrayals of "heretical" themes, and around the same time, a Pamphleteer named Robert Greene accused Marlowe of heresy and atheism. According to Greene, Marlowe drew attention to inconsistencies in the Bible, a charge that placed him in very grave danger. Thomas Kyd, a playwright and former roommate of Marlowe's, was also arrested on the charge of atheism and, under torture, implicated Marlowe, who was not immediately arrested. The Privy Council continued to gather information on him, however, especially after he gave some lectures on the subject of atheism.

Richard Baines, the other person involved in the earlier counterfeiting scheme, wrote a document titled, "Note Containing the opinion of one Christopher Marly Concerning his Damnable Judgement of Religion, and scorn of God's Word." This paper was intended to disgrace Marlowe and cause his imprisonment, but the authorities again failed to arrest him.

Marlowe would be dead within three days, however, giving rise to the belief that his death was a deliberate murder by the British government. He was involved in a barroom brawl on May 30, 1593, and stabbed in the eye, a wound that killed him. The men at his table were known to be, at least superficially, affiliated with the government, and Queen Elizabeth pardoned the man who actually stabbed him, Ingram Frizer, about two weeks after Marlowe's death.

Christopher Marlowe is one of the English language's long-overlooked and under-appreciated writers. Had it not been for Shakespeare's genius, Marlowe would probably have been considered the greatest Elizabethan playwright.

READING POINTERS

Reading Pointers for Sharper Insights

There are many versions and interpretations of the play, *The Tragical History of Dr. Faustus*, written by Christopher Marlowe in the late 1500s. The basic story, however, remains consistent throughout all the versions. The play is based on an old legend regarding Dr. Faustus, a man of knowledge and excessive pride, who sells his soul to the devil to gain power and knowledge of the universe.

Dr. Faustus is a drama, meaning that it was meant to be performed, rather than read as a novel. The following information will assist you in reading the play:

- Marlowe was an English playwright, so the dialect is Elizabethan, which can be a challenge to read and comprehend. Sidebar notes and the glossary will be helpful in deciphering the text.
- Latin words and phrases are used liberally, as was common during that time. Aside from the passages that seem to require the use of Latin (e.g., Catholic prayer), Marlowe seems to use Latin to emphasis a point. We have provided translations.
- The play incorporates elements of comedy. While you are reading, take note of the comical scenes. Sometimes a comedic scene can provide a break from the intensity of the serious scene that precedes it, a technique known as *comic relief*. Other times comedy is used to mask a serious or sensitive issue. Comedy is also used at face value, purely for entertainment purposes.
- Aside from Faustus and Mephistophilis, the characters in the play are flat—undeveloped, one-dimensional. It's possible that Marlowe did this to ensure that the focus stays on the main characters and to use the other characters as symbols (e.g., good, evil, politics, compassion, beauty, ignorance, etc.).

Marlowe's *Dr. Faustus* is a product of the Renaissance—a time of rebirth from the Medieval period. As you read *Dr. Faustus*, note the following characteristics of the Renaissance that are reflected in the story:

- explosive growth of knowledge
- improvement in literacy across the classes
- the rise of Renaissance Individualism, which encouraged people to better themselves and pursue personal fulfillment
- a lessening of the power of the Catholic Church due to the Protestant Reformation, which created political changes and conflicts
- the belief and the practice of magic, despite advances in science

Marlowe uses many allusions in the play. Note that the allusions illuminate the transitional nature of the Renaissance—the blending of old beliefs with new ideas and knowledge. Look for these allusions throughout the play and consider the purpose of their usage:

- biblical stories
- figures and stories in Greek mythology
- famous writers, poets, physicians, alchemists, and magicians from antiquity
- Spanish rule

The primary motif of the play is the conflict between good and evil. There are, however, other motifs that permeate the story of *Dr. Faustus*:

- Knowledge and Power—Knowledge is powerful, especially during the Renaissance, when knowledge was becoming more accessible to people, allowing them to improve their status in life. Knowledge and power can be used to help others or for personal gain. Faustus' motivation for pursuing knowledge and power, the method he uses to obtain them, and the consequences of his actions form the crux of the play.

- Old Testament vs. New Testament—Between the two, there is a difference in how God is viewed regarding the concept of sin and redemption. In the Old Testament, God punishes sinners. In the New Testament, God is forgiving. Faustus' view of sin is based on a misinterpretation of Jerome's Bible; this is a major factor in the decisions he makes.

- Christian Beliefs vs. The Practice of Magic—People of that time were very religious and quite superstitious. How does the lure of magic affect the various characters in the play? In particular, note how the "religious" characters respond to magic.

- The Duality of Humans—There are elements of good and bad in all of us. As the play unfolds, Faustus struggles internally with this duality, and it creates doubt about the choices he's made. Each of us has personality traits that have the power to affect the balance of our nature. Faustus is not inherently evil, but his excessive pride, greed, selfishness, and weakness of character cloud his judgment, causing him to make poor decisions. As you read the play, be aware of the moments where Faustus struggles with this duality.

After reading both the biography of Christopher Marlowe and *The Tragical History of Dr. Faustus*, you may find interesting parallels between Marlowe and Faustus.

DRAMATIS PERSONAE.

THE POPE.
CARDINAL OF LORRAIN.
EMPEROR OF GERMANY.
DUKE OF VANHOLT.
FAUSTUS.
VALDES,
CORNELIUS, } Friends to FAUSTUS.
WAGNER, Servant to FAUSTUS.
Clown.
ROBIN.
RALPH.
Vintner, Horse-Courser, Knight, Old Man, Scholars, Friars, and
    Attendants.

DUCHESS OF VANHOLT.

LUCIFER.
BELZEBUB.
MEPHISTOPHILIS.
Good Angel.
Evil Angel.
The Seven Deadly Sins.
Devils.
Spirits in the shape of ALEXANDER THE GREAT, of his Paramour, and
    of HELEN OF TROY.

CHORUS.

CHORUS.

Enter CHORUS.

CHORUS. Not marching now in fields of Thrasimene, *] not war*
    Where Mars† did mate[1] the Carthaginians;†   [1]defeat
    Nor sporting in the dalliance of love, *Not about*
    In courts of kings where state is overturned; *war + love or the stuff may performe*
5   Nor in the pomp of proud audacious deeds,
    Intends our Muse to vaunt her heavenly verse
    Only this, gentlemen,—we must perform *only going to talk about Faustus*
    The form of Faustus' fortunes, good or bad:
    To patient judgments we appeal our plaud,[2] *be patient*   [2]applause
10   And speak for Faustus in his infancy. *Not about bats*
    Now is he born, his parents base of stock, *common*
    In Germany, within a town called Rhodes: *went to school in wertdaberg*
    Of riper years, to Wertenberg he went,
    Whereas his kinsmen chiefly brought him up.
15   So soon he profits in divinity, *Scholar in christinity*
    The fruitful plot of scholarism graced,[3]   [3]academic learning
    That shortly he was graced with doctor's name, *given PHD*
    Excelling all whose sweet delight disputes *became too concided*
    In heavenly matters of theology;
20   Till swollen with cunning, of a self-conceit,
    His waxen wings† did mount above his reach,
    And, melting, Heavens conspired his overthrow;
    For, falling to a devilish exercise,
    And glutted now with learning's golden gifts,
25   He surfeits[4] upon cursed necromancy;[5] *gave into cursed magic*   [4]fills to excess
    Nothing so sweet as magic is to him,   [5]magic; the dark arts
    Which he prefers before his chiefest bliss:
    And this the man that in his study sits! *prefers over relion* [*Exit.*] *devine belief in magic*

---

†Terms marked in the text with (†) can be looked up in the Glossary
  for additional information.

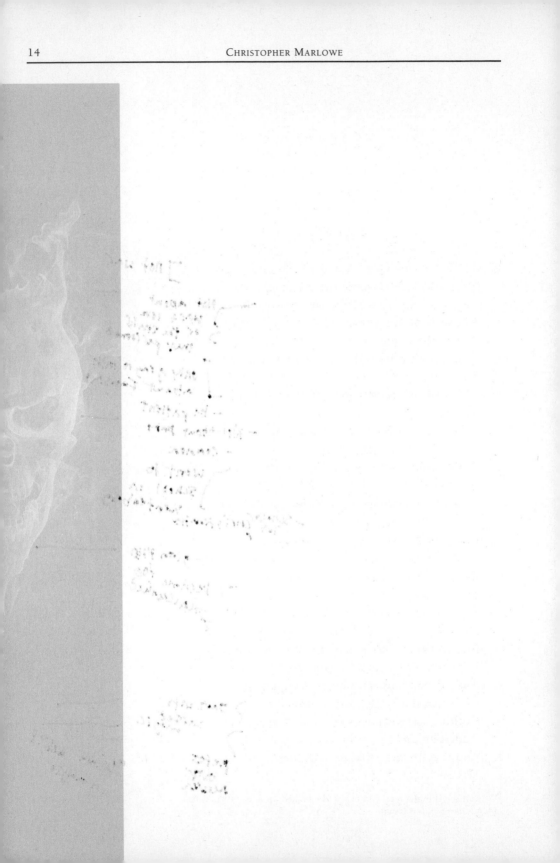

SCENE I.

SCENE I.

FAUSTUS *in his Study.*

FAUSTUS. Settle thy studies, Faustus, and begin
    To sound the depth of that thou wilt profess;[1]   [1]teach
    Having commenced, be a divine in show,
    Yet level[2] at the end of every art,   [2]aim
5   And live and die in Aristotle's works.
    Sweet Analytics,[3] 'tis thou hast ravished me!   [*Reads.*]   [3]the science of
    Bene disserere est finis logices.‡   logical analysis
    Is, to dispute well, logic's chiefest end?
    Affords this art no greater miracle?
10   Then read no more; thou hast attained that end;
    A greater subject fitteth Faustus' wit:
    Bid *Oncaymaeon*‡ farewell, Galen† come,
    Seeing, *Ubi desinit Philosophus, ibi incipit Medicus:*‡
    Be a physician, Faustus; heap up gold,
15   And be eternised[4] for some wondrous cure.   [*Reads.*] [4]made eternally
    Summum bonum medicinae sanitas,‡   famous
    The end of physic is our body's health.
    Why, Faustus, hast thou not attained that end?
    Is not thy common talk sound aphorisms?
20   Are not thy bills[5] hung up as monuments,   [5]announcements
    Whereby whole cities have escaped the plague,
    And thousand desperate maladies been eased?
    Yet art thou still but Faustus, and a man.
    Wouldst thou make men to live eternally,
25   Or, being dead, raise them to life again,
    Then this profession were to be esteemed.
    Physic, farewell!—Where is Justinian?†   [*Reads.*]
    Si una eademque res legatur duobus, alter rem,
    alter valorem rei, &c.‡

‡Terms marked in the text with (‡) can be looked up in the Latin Glossary
  for additional information.

[Handwritten annotations: "He has studied everything Aristotle has studied. Now studied. Teach others"; "Bound by Aris. teachings"; "he knows of something better he could be a dr. / physician + makes the forever bldm helped others"; "A dispute well is the purpose of logic / he mastered all logic"; "he saved whole cities from the plague"; "What is the law — 1 person gets the thing, the other values it"]

30   A pretty case of paltry legacies!   [*Reads.*]
      Exhaereditare filium non potest pater, nisi, &c.[†]
      Such is the subject of the institute,
      And universal body of the law:
      This study fits a mercenary drudge,
35   Who aims at nothing but external trash;
      Too servile and illiberal for me.
      When all is done, divinity is best:
      Jerome's Bible,[†] Faustus; view it well.   [*Reads.*]
      Stipendium peccati mors est. Ha! *Stipendium, &c.*[†]
40   The reward of sin is death. That's hard.   [*Reads.*]
      *Si peccasse negamus fallimur et nulla est in nobis
          veritas*[†]
      If we say that we have no sin, we deceive ourselves,
      and there's no truth in us. Why then, belike we
45   must sin, and so consequently die.
      Ay, we must die an everlasting death.
      What doctrine call you this, *Che sera, sera,*[†]
      What will be shall be? Divinity, adieu!
      These metaphysics of magicians
50   And necromantic books are heavenly:
      Lines, circles, scenes, letters, and characters:
      Ay, these are those that Faustus most desires.
      O, what a world of profit and delight,
      Of power, of honour, of omnipotence,
55   Is promised to the studious artisan!
      All things that move between the quiet poles
      Shall be at my command. Emperors and kings
      Are but obeyed in their several provinces,
      Nor can they raise the wind, or rend the clouds;
60   But his dominion that exceeds[6] in this,
      Stretcheth as far as doth the mind of man;
      A sound magician is a mighty god:
      Here, Faustus, tire thy brains to gain a deity.
      Wagner!

                    Enter WAGNER.

65   Wagner, commend me to my dearest friends,
      The German Valdes[†] and Cornelius;[†]
      Request them earnestly to visit me.

[6]surpasses

WAGNER. I will, sir.   [*Exit.*]

FAUSTUS. Their conference will be a greater help to me
70   Than all my labours, plod I ne'er so fast.

                Enter Good Angel *and* Evil Angel.

GOOD ANGEL. O, Faustus! lay that damned book aside,
        And gaze not upon it, lest it tempt thy soul,
        And heap God's heavy wrath upon thy head!
        Read, read the Scriptures:—that is blasphemy.

75 EVIL ANGEL. Go forward, Faustus, in that famous art,
        Wherein all Nature's treasure is contained:
        Be thou on earth as Jove† is in the sky,
        Lord and commander of these elements.
                                        [*Exeunt* Angels.]

FAUSTUS. How am I glutted with conceit⁷ of this!   ⁷ideas
80   Shall I make spirits fetch me what I please,
        Resolve me of all ambiguities,
        Perform what desperate enterprise I will?
        I'll have them fly to India for gold,
        Ransack the ocean for orient pearl,
85   And search all corners of the new-found world
        For pleasant fruits and princely delicates;
        I'll have them read me strange philosophy,
        And tell the secrets of all foreign kings:
        I'll have them wall all Germany with brass,
90   And make the swift Rhine circle fair Wertenberg;
        I'll have them fill the public schools with silk,
        Wherewith the students shall be bravely clad;
        I'll levy soldiers with the coin they bring,
        And chase the Prince of Parma† from our land,
95   And reign sole king of all the provinces;
        Yea, stranger engines for the brunt of war,
        Than was the fiery keel at Antwerp's bridge,†
        I'll make my servile spirits to invent.

Enter VALDES *and* CORNELIUS.

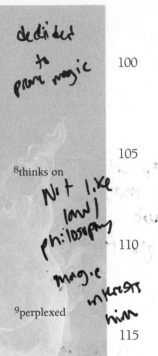

           Come, German Valdes, and Cornelius,
100   And make me blest with your sage conference.
           Valdes, sweet Valdes, and Cornelius,
           Know that your words have won me at the last
           To practice magic and concealed arts:
           Yet not your words only, but mine own fantasy
105   That will receive no object, for my head
           But ruminates[8] on necromantic skill.
           Philosophy is odious and obscure,
           Both law and physic are for petty wits;
           Divinity is basest of the three,
110   Unpleasant, harsh, contemptible, and vile:
           'tis magic, magic, that hath ravished me.
           Then, gentle friends, aid me in this attempt;
           And I that have with concise syllogisms
           Gravelled[9] the pastors of the German church,
115   And made the flowering pride of Wertenberg
           Swarm to my problems, as the infernal spirits
           On sweet Musaeus† when he came to hell,
           Will be as cunning as Agrippa was,
           Whose shadow made all Europe honour him.

120   VALDES. Faustus, these books, thy wit, and our
               experience,
           Shall make all nations to canonise us.
           As Indian Moors† obey their Spanish lords,
           So shall the spirits of every element
125   Be always serviceable to us three;
           Like lions shall they guard us when we please;
           Like Almain rutters[10] with their horsemen's staves,
           Or Lapland giants,† trotting by our sides;
           Sometimes like women or unwedded maids,
130   Shadowing more beauty in their airy brows
           Than have the white breasts of the queen of love:
           From Venice shall they drag huge argosies,
           And from America the golden fleece
           That yearly stuffs old Philip's treasury;†
135   If learned Faustus will be resolute.

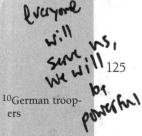

[8] thinks on

[9] perplexed

[10] German troopers

FAUSTUS. Valdes, as resolute am I in this
          As thou to live; therefore object it not.

CORNELIUS. The miracles that magic will perform
          Will make thee vow to study nothing else.
140   He that is grounded in astrology,
          Enriched with tongues,[11] well seen[12] in minerals,
          Hath all the principles magic doth require.
          Then doubt not, Faustus, but to be renowned,
          And more frequented[13] for this mystery
145   Than heretofore the Delphian Oracle.†
          The spirits tell me they can dry the sea,
          And fetch the treasure of all foreign wrecks,
      Ay, all the wealth that our forefathers hid
          Within the massy entrails of the earth;
150   Then tell me, Faustus, what shall we three want?

FAUSTUS. Nothing, Cornelius! O this cheers my soul!
          Come, show me some demonstrations magical,
          That I may conjure in some bushy grove,
          And have these joys in full possession.

155 VALDES. Then haste thee to some solitary grove,
          And bear wise Bacon's† and Albanus'† works,
          The Hebrew Psalter, and New Testament;
          And whatsoever else is requisite
          We will inform thee ere our conference cease.

160 CORNELIUS. Valdes, first let him know the words of art;
          And then, all other ceremonies learned,
          Faustus may try his cunning by himself.

VALDES. First I'll instruct thee in the rudiments,
          And then wilt thou be perfecter than I.

165 FAUSTUS. Then come and dine with me, and after meat,
          We'll canvas every quiddity[14] thereof;
          For ere I sleep I'll try what I can do:
          This night I'll conjure tho' I die therefore.

                                        [*Exeunt.*]

[11]languages

[12]versed

[13]visited

[14]detail

[Handwritten margin notes:]
V + E encourage Faustus to join him
Knows how to do magic (back ground)
the spirits can do anything so do what you want
His practise magic?
in form others
instruct them
we'll work out details

SCENE II.

Enter two Scholars.

FIRST SCHOLAR. I wonder what's become of Faustus that
was wont to make our school ring with *sic probo*? (this I prove)

SECOND SCHOLAR. That shall we know, for see here
comes his boy.

Enter WAGNER. — Fauts's servant

5 FIRST SCHOLAR. How now, sirrah! Where's thy master?

WAGNER. God in heaven knows!

SECOND SCHOLAR. Why, dost not thou know?

WAGNER. Yes, I know. But that follows not.

Wagner knows where he is, but doesn't know what follows

FIRST SCHOLAR. Go to, sirrah! leave your jesting, and tell
10   us where he is.

WAGNER. That follows not necessary by force of argument,
that you, being licentiates, should stand upon: therefore
acknowledge your error and be attentive.

SECOND SCHOLAR. Why, didst thou not say thou
15   knewest?

WAGNER. Have you any witness on't?

FIRST SCHOLAR. Yes, sirrah, I heard you.

WAGNER. Ask my fellows if I be a thief.

SECOND SCHOLAR. Well, you will not tell us?

20 WAGNER. Yes, sir, I will tell you; yet, if you were not
dunces, you would never ask me such a question; for
is not he *corpus naturale*?[‡] and is not that *mobile*?[‡] then
wherefore should you ask me such a question? But
that I am by nature phlegmatic,[1][†] slow to wrath, and
25 prone to lechery (to love, I would say), it were not for
you to come within forty foot of the place of execution, although I do not doubt to see you both hanged
the next sessions. Thus having triumphed over you, I
will set my countenance like a precisian,[2] and begin
30 to speak thus:—Truly, my dear brethren,[3] my master
is within at dinner, with Valdes and Cornelius, as this
wine, if it could speak, would inform your worships;
and so, the Lord bless you, preserve you, and keep you,
my dear brethren, my dear brethren.   [*Exit.*]

35 FIRST SCHOLAR. Nay, then, I fear he is fallen into that
damned Art for which they two are infamous through
the world.

SECOND SCHOLAR. Were he a stranger, and not allied to
me, yet should I grieve for him. But come, let us go and
40 inform the Rector, and see if he by his grave counsel
can reclaim him.

FIRST SCHOLAR. O, but I fear me nothing can reclaim
him.

SECOND SCHOLAR. Yet let us try what we can do.
     [*Exeunt.*]

[1] impassive

[2] Punish

[3] brothers, as in associates

Handwritten marginalia:
Why would you ask me where he is, he's / moving person
doesn't want to kill him / Punish he is
Wagner thinks he's an idiot
let's try to get him to stop magic

SCENE III.

Enter FAUSTUS *to* conjure

FAUSTUS. Now that the gloomy shadow of the earth
    Longing to view Orion's drizzling look,
    Leaps from the antarctic world unto the sky,
    And dims the welkin[1] with her pitchy breath,
5   Faustus, begin thine incantations,
    And try if devils will obey thy hest,
    Seeing thou hast prayed and sacrificed to them.
    Within this circle is Jehovah's name,
    Forward and backward anagrammatised,
10   The breviated names of holy saints,
    Figures of every adjunct[2] to the Heavens,
    And characters of signs and erring stars,[3]
    By which the spirits are enforced to rise:
    Then fear not, Faustus, but be resolute,
15   And try the uttermost magic can perform.
    Sint mihi dei Acherontis propitii! Valeat numen triplex
    Jehovoe! Ignei, aerii, aquatani spiritus, salvete!
    Orientis princeps Belzebub, inferni ardentis monarcha,
    et Demogorgon, propitiamus vos, ut appareat et surgat
20   *Mephistophilis. Quid tu moraris? per Jehovam, Gehennam,*
    et consecratam aquam quam nunc spargo, signumque
    crucis quod nunc facio, et per vota nostra, ipse nunc
    surgat nobis dicatus Mephistophilis![‡]

Enter MEPHISTOPHILIS.

    I charge thee to return and change thy shape;
25   Thou art too ugly to attend on me.
    Go, and return an old Franciscan friar;
    That holy shape becomes a devil best.

[1]heavens

[2]connection

[3]planets

23

[*Exit* MEPHISTOPHILIS.]

I see there's virtue in my heavenly words;
Who would not be proficient in this art?
30 How pliant is this Mephistophilis,
Full of obedience and humility!
Such is the force of magic and my spells:
Now Faustus, thou art conjuror laureat,
That canst command great Mephistophilis:
35 *Quin regis Mephistophilis fratris imagine.*†

Re-enter MEPHISTOPHILIS *like a* Franciscan Friar.

MEPHIST. Now, Faustus, what would'st thou have me
    to do?

FAUSTUS. I charge thee wait upon me whilst I live,
    To do whatever Faustus shall command,
40   Be it to make the moon drop from her sphere,
    Or the ocean to overwhelm the world.

MEPHIST. I am a servant to great Lucifer,
    And may not follow thee without his leave
    No more than he commands must we perform.

45 FAUSTUS. Did not he charge thee to appear to me?

MEPHIST. No, I came hither of mine own accord.

FAUSTUS. Did not my conjuring speeches raise thee?
    Speak.

MEPHIST. That was the cause, but yet *per accidens*;†
50   For when we hear one rack⁴ the name of God,
    Abjure the Scriptures and his Saviour Christ,
    We fly in hope to get his glorious soul;
    Nor will we come, unless he use such means
    Whereby he is in danger to be damned:
55   Therefore the shortest cut for conjuring
    Is stoutly to abjure the Trinity,
    And pray devoutly to the Prince of Hell.

⁴twist

FAUSTUS. So Faustus hath
      Already done; and holds this principle,
60   There is no chief but only Belzebub;
      To whom Faustus doth dedicate himself.
      This word "damnation" terrifies not him,
      For he confounds hell in Elysium;[5]
      His ghost be with the old philosophers!
65   But, leaving these vain trifles of men's souls,
      Tell me what is that Lucifer thy lord?

MEPHIST. Arch-regent and commander of all spirits.

FAUSTUS. Was not that Lucifer an angel once?

MEPHIST. Yes, Faustus, and most dearly loved of God.

70 FAUSTUS. How comes it then that he is prince of devils?

MEPHIST. O, by aspiring pride and insolence;
      For which God threw him from the face of Heaven.

FAUSTUS. And what are you that live with Lucifer?

MEPHIST. Unhappy spirits that fell with Lucifer,
75   Conspired against our God with Lucifer,
      And are for ever damned with Lucifer.

FAUSTUS. Where are you damned?

MEPHIST. In hell.

FAUSTUS. How comes it then that thou art out of hell?

80 MEPHIST. Why this is hell, nor am I out of it:
      Think'st thou that I who saw the face of God,
      And tasted the eternal joys of Heaven,
      Am not tormented with ten thousand hells,
      In being deprived of everlasting bliss?
85   O, Faustus! leave these frivolous demands,
      Which strike a terror to my fainting soul.

[5]Heaven and hell are indifferent to him.

(handwritten margin note:) Explains how Lucifer was kicked out of heaven

(handwritten margin note:) Warning him to leave.

FAUSTUS. What, is great Mephistophilis so passionate
    For being deprived of the joys of Heaven?
    Learn thou of Faustus manly fortitude,
90   And scorn those joys thou never shalt possess.
    Go bear these tidings to great Lucifer:
    Seeing Faustus hath incurred eternal death
    By desperate thoughts against Jove's deity,
    Say he surrenders up to him his soul,
95   So he will spare him four and twenty years,
    Letting him live in all voluptuousness;
    Having thee ever to attend on me;
    To give me whatsoever I shall ask,
    To tell me whatsoever I demand,
100   To slay mine enemies, and aid my friends,
    And always be obedient to my will.
    Go and return to mighty Lucifer,
    And meet me in my study at midnight,
[6]advise   And then resolve[6] me of thy master's mind.

Handwritten margin note: I'll sell my soul, space me 24 years be obedient to me

105 MEPHIST. I will, Faustus.   [*Exit.*]

FAUSTUS. Had I as many souls as there be stars,
    I'd give them all for Mephistophilis.
    By him I'll be great Emperor of the world,
    And make a bridge thorough the moving air,
110   To pass the ocean with a band of men:
    I'll join the hills that bind the Afric shore,
    And make that country continent to Spain,
    And both contributory to my crown.
    The Emperor shall not live but by my leave,
115   Nor any potentate of Germany.
    Now that I have obtained what I desire,
[7]research   I'll live in speculation[7] of this art
    Till Mephistophilis return again.   [*Exit.*]

SCENE IV.

Enter WAGNER *and* Clown.

WAGNER. Sirrah, boy, come hither.

CLOWN. How, boy! Swowns,[1] boy! I hope you have seen many boys with such pickadevaunts[2] as I have; boy, quotha!

5 WAGNER. Tell me, sirrah, hast thou any comings in?

CLOWN. Ay, and goings out too. You may see else.

WAGNER. Alas, poor slave! see how poverty jesteth in his nakedness! the villain is bare and out of service, and so hungry that I know he would give his soul to the Devil or
10   a shoulder of mutton, though 'twere blood-raw.

CLOWN. How! My soul to the Devil for a shoulder of mutton, though 'twere blood-raw! Not so, good friend. By'r Lady, I had need have it well roasted, and good sauce to it, if I pay so dear.

15 WAGNER. Well, wilt thou serve us, and I'll make thee go like *Qui mihi discipulus?*‡

CLOWN. How, in verse?

WAGNER. No, sirrah; in beaten silk and stavesacre.[3]

CLOWN. How, how, Knaves acre![4] I, I thought that was all
20   the land his father left him. Do you hear? I would be sorry to rob you of your living.

[1] an altered form of Zounds (God's wounds)

[2] pointy beards

[3] a kind of larkspur, the seeds of which are used to kill head lice

[4] a London street with a bad reputation

27

WAGNER. Sirrah, I say in stavesacre.

CLOWN. Oho! Oho! Stavesacre! Why, then, belike if I were your man I should be full of vermin.

25   WAGNER. So thou shalt, whether thou beest with me or no. But, sirrah, leave your jesting, and bind yourself presently unto me for seven years, or I'll turn all the lice about thee into familiars, and they shall tear thee in pieces.

30   CLOWN. Do you hear, sir? You may save that labour: they are too familiar with me already: swowns! they are as bold with my flesh as if they had paid for their meat and drink.

WAGNER. Well, do you hear, sirrah? Hold, take these
35   guilders.   [*Gives money.*]

CLOWN. Gridirons! what be they?

WAGNER. Why, French crowns.

CLOWN. Mass, but in the name of French crowns, a man were as good have as many English counters. And
40   what should I do with these?

WAGNER. Why, now, sirrah, thou art at an hour's warning, whensoever and wheresoever the Devil shall fetch thee.

CLOWN. No, no. Here, take your gridirons again.

45   WAGNER. Truly I'll none of them.

CLOWN. Truly but you shall.

WAGNER. Bear witness I gave them him.

CLOWN. Bear witness I give them you again.

WAGNER. Well, I will cause two devils presently to fetch thee
50   away.—Baliol and Belcher.

CLOWN. Let your Baliol and your Belcher come here, and
        I'll knock them, they were never so knocked since they
        were devils! say I should kill one of them, what would
        folks say? "Do you see yonder tall fellow in the round
55   slop?⁵—he has killed the devil." So I should be called
        Kill-devil all the parish over.

Enter two Devils: *the* Clown *runs up and down crying.*

WAGNER. Baliol and Belcher! Spirits, away!
                                    [*Exeunt* Devils.]

CLOWN. What, are they gone? A vengeance on them, they
        have vile long nails! There was a he-devil and a she-devil!
60   I'll tell you how you shall know them; all he-devils has
        horns, and all she-devils has clifts⁶ and cloven feet.

WAGNER. Well, sirrah, follow me.

CLOWN. But, do you hear—if I should serve you, would you
        teach me to raise up Banios and Belcheos?

65 WAGNER. I will teach thee to turn thyself to anything; to a
        dog, or a cat, or a mouse, or a rat, or anything.

CLOWN. How! a Christian fellow to a dog or a cat, a mouse
        or a rat! No, no, sir; if you turn me into anything, let it be
        in the likeness of a little pretty frisking flea, that I may be
70   here and there and everywhere: Oh, I'll tickle the pretty
        wenches' plackets; I'll be amongst them, i'faith.

WAGNER. Well, sirrah, come.

CLOWN. But, do you hear, Wagner?

WAGNER. How!—Baliol and Belcher!

⁵breeches; trousers

⁶cleft

CLOWN. O Lord! I pray, sir, let Banio and Belcher go
75   sleep.

WAGNER. Villain—call me Master Wagner, and let thy
left eye be Diametarily[7] fixed upon my right heel, with
quasi vestigiis nostris insistere.‡   [*Exit.*]

CLOWN. God forgive me, he speaks Dutch fustian. Well,
80   I'll follow him: I'll serve him, that's flat.
                           [*Exit.*]

[7]diametrically; opposite to

SCENE V.

FAUSTUS *discovered in his Study*.

FAUSTUS. Now, Faustus, must
    Thou needs be damned, and canst thou not be saved:
    What boots[1] it then to think of God or heaven?
    Away with such vain fancies, and despair:
5   Despair in God, and trust in Belzebub;
    Now go not backward: no, Faustus, be resolute:
    Why waver'st thou? O, something soundeth in mine
        ears
    "Abjure this magic, turn to God again!"
10   Ay, and Faustus will turn to God again.
    To God?——He loves thee not—
    The god thou serv'st is thine own appetite,
    Wherein is fixed the love of Belzebub;
    To him I'll build an altar and a church,
15   And offer lukewarm blood of new-born babes.

       Enter Good Angel *and* Evil Angel.

GOOD ANGEL. Sweet Faustus, leave that execrable[2] art.

FAUSTUS. Contrition, prayer, repentance! What of them?

GOOD ANGEL. O, they are means to bring thee unto
    Heaven!

20 EVIL ANGEL. Rather illusions—fruits of lunacy,
    That makes men foolish that do trust them most.

GOOD ANGEL. Sweet Faustus, think of Heaven and
    heavenly things.

[1] are the advantages

[2] detestable

31

EVIL ANGEL. No, Faustus, think of honour and of
       wealth.

                                          [*Exeunt* Angels.]

3 respected men

25 FAUSTUS. Of wealth!
       Why, the signiory[3] of Embden† shall be mine.
       When Mephistophilis shall stand by me,
       What god can hurt thee? Faustus, thou art safe:
       Cast no more doubts. Come, Mephistophilis,
30   And bring glad tidings from great Lucifer; —
       Is't not midnight? Come, Mephistophilis;
       Veni, veni, Mephistophile!‡

                Enter MEPHISTOPHILIS.

       Now tell me, what says Lucifer thy lord?

       MEPHIST. That I shall wait on Faustus whilst he lives,
35   So he will buy my service with his soul.

       FAUSTUS. Already Faustus hath hazarded that for thee.

       MEPHIST. But, Faustus, thou must bequeath it solemnly,
       And write a deed of gift with thine own blood,
       For that security craves great Lucifer.
40   If thou deny it, I will back to hell.

       FAUSTUS. Stay, Mephistophilis! and tell me what good
       Will my soul do thy lord?

       MEPHIST. Enlarge his kingdom.

       FAUSTUS. Is that the reason why he tempts us thus?

45   MEPHIST. *Solamen miseris socios habuisse doloris.*‡

       FAUSTUS. Why, have you any pain that tortures others?

       MEPHIST. As great as have the human souls of men.
       But tell me, Faustus, shall I have thy soul?

And I will be thy slave, and wait on thee,
50   And give thee more than thou hast wit to ask.

FAUSTUS. Ay, Mephistophilis, I give it thee.   *yes, I give my soul*

MEPHIST. Then, Faustus, stab thine arm courageously
        And bind thy soul that at some certain day
        Great Lucifer may claim it as his own;
55   And then be thou as great as Lucifer.

FAUSTUS. [*Stabbing his arm.*] Lo, Mephistophilis, for love of
            thee,
        I cut mine arm, and with my proper blood
        Assure my soul to be great Lucifer's,
60   Chief lord and regent of perpetual night!
        View here the blood that trickles from mine arm,
        And let it be propitious[4] for my wish.   [4]favorable

MEPHIST. But, Faustus, thou must
        Write it in manner of a deed of gift.

65 FAUSTUS. Ay, so I will. [*Writes.*] But, Mephistophilis,   *blood thickness*
        My blood congeals, and I can write no more.   *– fire to melt*

MEPHIST. I'll fetch thee fire to dissolve it straight.   [*Exit.*]

FAUSTUS. What might the staying of my blood portend?   *doubts himself.*
        Is it unwilling I should write this bill?   *Should I not?*
70   Why streams it not, that I may write afresh?   *What does my*
        Faustus gives to thee his soul. Ah, there it stayed!   *blood say*
        Why should'st thou not? Is not thy soul thine own?
        Then write again, *Faustus gives to thee his soul.*

        Re-enter MEPHISTOPHILIS *with a chafer of coals.*

MEPHIST. Here's fire. Come, Faustus, set it on.

75 FAUSTUS. So now the blood begins to clear again;
        Now will I make an end immediately.   [*Writes.*]

MEPHIST. O, what will not I do to obtain his soul?

[*Aside.*]

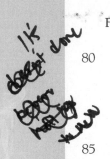

FAUSTUS. *Consummatum est:*‡ this bill is ended,
 And Faustus hath bequeathed his soul to Lucifer.
80 But what is this inscription on mine arm?
 Homo, fuge!‡ Whither should I fly?
 If unto God, he'll throw me down to hell.
 My senses are deceived; here's nothing writ:—
 I see it plain; here in this place is writ
85 *Homo, fuge!* Yet shall not Faustus fly.

MEPHIST. I'll fetch him somewhat to delight his mind.

[*Exit.*]

Re-enter MEPHISTOPHILIS *with* Devils, *who give crowns
and rich apparel to* FAUSTUS, *dance, and depart.*

FAUSTUS. Speak, Mephistophilis, what means this show?

MEPHIST. Nothing, Faustus, but to delight thy mind
 withal,
90 And to show thee what magic can perform.

FAUSTUS. But may I raise up spirits when I please?

MEPHIST. Ay, Faustus, and do greater things than these.

FAUSTUS. Then there's enough for a thousand souls.
 Here, Mephistophilis, receive this scroll,
95 A deed of gift of body and of soul:
 But yet conditionally that thou perform
 All articles prescribed between us both.

MEPHIST. Faustus, I swear by hell and Lucifer
 To effect all promises between us made.

100 FAUSTUS. Then hear me read them: *On these conditions
 following. First, that Faustus may be a spirit in form and
 substance. Secondly, that Mephistophilis shall be his ser-*

vant, and at his command. Thirdly, that Mephistophilis shall
do for him and bring him whatsoever he desires. Fourthly,
105   *that he shall be in his chamber or house invisible. Lastly,*
that he shall appear to the said John Faustus, at all times,
and in what form or shape soever he pleases. I, John Faustus,
of Wertenberg, Doctor, by these presents do give both body
and soul to Lucifer, Prince of the East, and his minister,
110   *Mephistophilis: and furthermore grant unto them, that*
twenty-four years being expired, the articles above-written
inviolate, full power to fetch or carry the said John Faustus,
body and soul, flesh, blood, or goods, into their habitation
wheresoever. By me, John Faustus.

115   MEPHIST. Speak, Faustus, do you deliver this as your deed?

FAUSTUS. Ay, take it, and the Devil give thee good on't!

MEPHIST. Now, Faustus, ask what thou wilt.

FAUSTUS. First will I question with thee about hell.
        Tell me where is the place that men call hell?

120   MEPHIST. Under the heavens.

FAUSTUS. Ay, but whereabout?

MEPHIST. Within the bowels of these elements,
        Where we are tortured and remain for ever;
        Hell hath no limits, nor is circumscribed
125   In one self place; for where we are is hell,
        And where hell is there must we ever be:
        And, to conclude, when all the world dissolves,
        And every creature shall be purified,
        All places shall be hell that is not Heaven.

130   FAUSTUS. Come, I think hell's a fable.

MEPHIST. Ay, think so still, till experience change thy mind.

FAUSTUS. Why, think'st thou, then, that Faustus shall be
        damned?

MEPHIST. Ay, of necessity, for here's the scroll
135   Wherein thou hast given thy soul to Lucifer.

[handwritten: doesn't believe will go to Hell]

FAUSTUS. Ay, and body too; but what of that?
          Think'st thou that Faustus is so fond to imagine
          That, after this life, there is any pain?
          Tush; these are trifles and mere old wives' tales.

140 MEPHIST. But, Faustus, I am an instance to prove the
                    contrary,
          For I am damned, and am now in hell.

FAUSTUS. How! now in hell?
          Nay, an this be hell, I'll willingly be damned here;
145   What? walking, disputing, &c.?
          But, leaving off this, let me have a wife,
          The fairest maid in Germany;
          For I am wanton and lascivious,
          And cannot live without a wife.

150 MEPHIST. How—a wife?
          I prithee,[5] Faustus, talk not of a wife.

[5] pray thee (please)

FAUSTUS. Nay, sweet Mephistophilis, fetch me one, for I
          will have one.

MEPHIST. Well—thou wilt have one? Sit there till I come:
155   I'll fetch thee a wife in the Devil's name.   [*Exit.*]

          Re-enter MEPHISTOPHILIS *with a* Devil
          dressed like a woman, with fireworks.

MEPHIST. Tell me, Faustus, how dost thou like thy wife?

FAUSTUS. A plague on her for a hot whore!

[handwritten: Hypocrisy]

MEPHIST. Tut, Faustus,
          Marriage is but a ceremonial toy;
160   If thou lovest me, think no more of it.
          I'll cull thee out the fairest courtesans,
          And bring them every morning to thy bed;

[handwritten: He isn't following through w/ Faustus bid]

{ She whom thine eye shall like, thy heart shall have,
  Be she as chaste as was Penelope,†
165 As wise as Saba,† or as beautiful
  As was bright Lucifer before his fall.
  Here, take this book, peruse it thoroughly:

[Gives a book.]

Skrts to Kell Fuustus what to do (handwritten annotation)

The iterating[6] of these lines brings gold;

[6]speaking

The framing of this circle on the ground
170 Brings whirlwinds, tempests, thunder and lightning;
  Pronounce this thrice devoutly to thyself,
  And men in armour shall appear to thee,
  Ready to execute what thou desir'st.

FAUSTUS. Thanks, Mephistophilis: yet fain[7] would I have a

[7] eager; pleased

175 book wherein I might behold all spells and incantations,
  that I might raise up spirits when I please.

MEPHIST. Here they are, in this book.   *[Turns to them.]*

FAUSTUS. Now would I have a book where I might see all
  characters and planets of the heavens, that I might know
180 their motions and dispositions.

MEPHIST. Here they are too.   *[Turns to them.]*

FAUSTUS. Nay, let me have one book more,—and then I have
  done,—wherein I might see all plants, herbs, and trees,
  that grow upon the earth.

185 MEPHIST. Here they be.

FAUSTUS. O, thou art deceived.

MEPHIST. Tut, I warrant thee.   *[Turns to them. Exeunt.]*

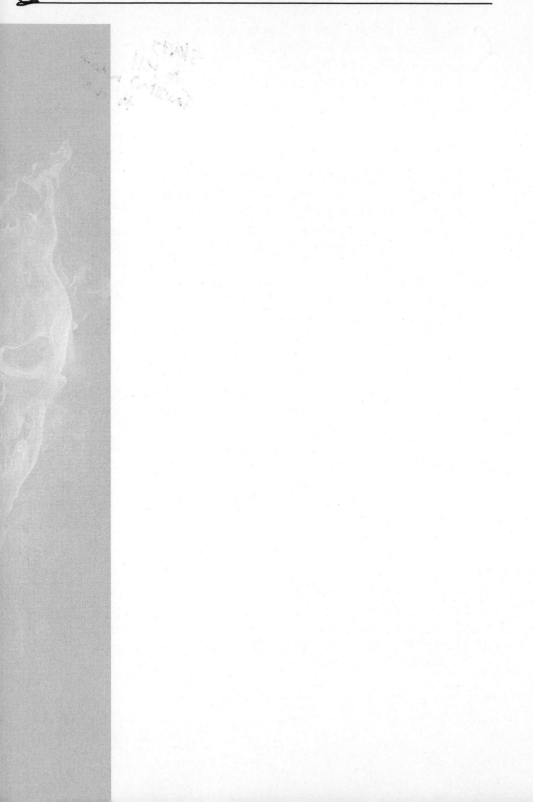

SCENE VI.

Enter FAUSTUS *and* MEPHISTOPHILIS.

FAUSTUS. When I behold the heavens, then I repent,
And curse thee, wicked Mephistophilis,
Because thou hast deprived me of those joys.

MEPHIST. Why, Faustus,
5   Thinkest thou Heaven is such a glorious thing?
I tell thee, 'tis not half so fair as thou,
Or any man that breathes on earth.

FAUSTUS. How prov'st thou that?

MEPHIST. 'Twas made for man, therefore is man more
10   excellent.

FAUSTUS. If it were made for man, 'twas made for me;
I will renounce this magic and repent.

Enter Good Angel *and* Evil Angel.

GOOD ANGEL. Faustus, repent; yet God will pity thee.

EVIL ANGEL. Thou art a spirit; God can not pity thee.

15 FAUSTUS. Who buzzeth in mine ears I am a spirit?
Be I a devil, yet God may pity me;
Ay, God will pity me if I repent.

EVIL ANGEL. Ay, but Faustus never shall repent.

[*Exeunt* Angels.]

39

FAUSTUS. My heart's so hardened, I cannot repent.
20   Scarce can I name salvation, faith, or heaven,
         But fearful echoes thunder in mine ears
         "Faustus, thou art damned!" Then swords, and
               knives,
         Poison, gun, halters, and envenomed steel
25   Are laid before me to despatch myself,
         And long ere this I should have slain myself,
         Had not sweet pleasure conquered deep despair.
         Have not I made blind Homer† sing to me
         Of Alexander's† love and Oenon's† death?
30   And hath not he that built the walls of Thebes†
         With ravishing sound of his melodious harp,
         Made music with my Mephistophilis?
         Why should I die then, or basely despair?
         I am resolved: Faustus shall ne'er repent.—
35   Come, Mephistophilis, let us dispute again,
         And argue of divine astrology.
         Tell me, are there many heavens above the moon?
         Are all celestial bodies but one globe,
         As is the substance of this centric earth?

40 MEPHIST. As are the elements, such are the spheres,
         Mutually folded in each other's orb,
         And, Faustus,
¹axle; rod   All jointly move upon one axletree,¹
²boundary   Whose terminine² is termed the world's wide pole;
45   Nor are the names of Saturn, Mars, or Jupiter
³pretended   Feigned,³ but are erring stars.

    FAUSTUS. But tell me, have they all one motion
             both, *situ et tempore*?‡

    MEPHIST. All jointly move from east to west in twenty-
50   four hours upon the poles of the world; but differ in
         their motion upon the poles of the zodiac.

    FAUSTUS. Tush!
         These slender trifles Wagner can decide;
         Hath Mephistophilis no greater skill?

55   Who knows not the double motion of the planets?
        The first is finished in a natural day;
        The second thus: as Saturn in thirty years; Jupiter in
        twelve; Mars in four; the Sun, Venus, and Mercury in
        a year; the Moon in twenty-eight days. Tush, these are
60   freshmen's suppositions. But, tell me, hath every sphere a
        dominion or *intelligentia*?[‡]

MEPHIST. Ay.

FAUSTUS. How many heavens, or spheres, are there?

MEPHIST. Nine: the seven planets, the firmament, and the
65   empyreal heaven.

FAUSTUS. Well, resolve me in this question: Why have we
        not conjunctions, oppositions, aspects, eclipses, all at one
        time, but in some years we have more, in some less?

MEPHIST. *Per inæqualem motum respectu totius.*[‡]

70 FAUSTUS. Well, I am answered. Tell me who made the
        world?

MEPHIST. I will not.

FAUSTUS. Sweet Mephistophilis, tell me.

MEPHIST. Move me not, for I will not tell thee.

75 FAUSTUS. Villain, have I not bound thee to tell me any
        thing?

MEPHIST. Ay, that is not against our kingdom; but this is.
        Think thou on hell, Faustus, for thou art damned.

FAUSTUS. Think, Faustus, upon God that made the world.

80 MEPHIST. Remember this.   [*Exit.*]

FAUSTUS. Ay, go, <u>accursed spirit</u>, to ugly hell.
  'tis thou hast damned distressed Faustus' soul.
  Is't not too late?

    Re-enter Good Angel *and* Evil Angel.

EVIL ANGEL. <u>Too late.</u>

85 GOOD ANGEL. Never too late, if Faustus can repent.

EVIL ANGEL. If thou repent, devils shall tear thee in
  pieces.

GOOD ANGEL. Repent, and they shall never raze thy
  skin.   [*Exeunt* Angels.]

90 FAUSTUS. Ah, Christ, my Saviour,
  Seek to save distressed Faustus' soul!

    Enter LUCIFER, BELZEBUB, *and* MEPHISTOPHILIS.

LUCIFER. Christ cannot save thy soul, for he is just;
  There's none but I have interest in the same.

FAUSTUS. O, who art thou that look'st so terrible?

95 LUCIFER. I am Lucifer,
  And this is my companion-prince in hell.

FAUSTUS. O, Faustus, they are come to fetch away thy
  soul!

LUCIFER. We come to tell thee thou dost injure us;
100 Thou talk'st of Christ, contrary to thy promise:
  Thou shouldst not <u>think</u> of God: <u>think</u> of the devil,
  And of his dam too.

FAUSTUS. Nor will I henceforth: pardon me in this,
  And Faustus vows never to look to Heaven,
105 Never to name God, or to pray to him,

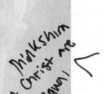

To burn his Scriptures, slay his ministers,
And make my spirits pull his churches down.

[handwritten: Intense hatred]

LUCIFER. Do so, and we will highly gratify thee. Faustus, we
are come from hell to show thee some pastime: sit down,
110   and thou shalt see all the Seven Deadly Sins appear in
their proper shapes.

[handwritten: forcing to view]

FAUSTUS. That sight will be as pleasing unto me,
As Paradise was to Adam, the first day
Of his creation.

[handwritten: he will be very pleased]

115 LUCIFER. Talk not of Paradise nor creation, but mark this
show: talk of the Devil, and nothing else: come away!

Enter the Seven Deadly Sins.

Now, Faustus, examine them of their several names and
dispositions.

FAUSTUS. What art thou—the first?

120 PRIDE. I am Pride. I disdain to have any parents. I am like
to Ovid's flea: I can creep into every corner of a wench;
sometimes, like a periwig, I sit upon her brow; or like
a fan of feathers, I kiss her lips; indeed I do—what do I
not? But, fie, what a scent is here! I'll not speak another
125   word, except the ground were perfumed, and covered
with cloth of arras.[4]

[handwritten: VIRTUES]

[handwritten: opposite = humility]

[handwritten: mainly associated w/ women]

[4]tapestry

FAUSTUS. What art thou—the second?

COVETOUSNESS. I am Covetousness, begotten of an old
churl in an old leathern bag; and, might I have my wish
130   I would desire that this house and all the people in it
were turned to gold, that I might lock you up in my good
chest. O, my sweet gold!

[handwritten: desire for wealthy possessions]

FAUSTUS. What art thou—the third?

[handwritten: opposite = charity]

[handwritten right margin: God sent Devil away to become more powerful]

VirMes

anger

WRATH. I am Wrath. I had neither father nor mother: I
135   leapt out of a lion's mouth when I was scarce half an
hour old; and ever since I have run up and down the
world with this case of rapiers, wounding myself when
I had nobody to fight withal. I was born in hell; and
look to it, for some of you shall be my father.

140 FAUSTUS. What art thou—the fourth?

Jealousy
of rich

ENVY. I am Envy, begotten of a chimney sweeper and an
oyster-wife. I cannot read, and therefore wish all books
were burnt. I am lean with seeing others eat. O that
there would come a famine through all the world, that
145   all might die, and I live alone! then thou should'st see
how fat I would be. But must thou sit, and I stand!
Come down with a vengeance!

FAUSTUS. Away, envious rascal! What art thou—the
fifth?

150 GLUTTONY. Who I, sir? I am Gluttony. My parents are
all dead, and the devil a penny they have left me, but
a bare pension, and that is thirty meals a day and ten
bevers,[5]—a small trifle to suffice nature. O, I come of
a royal parentage! My grandfather was a Gammon of
155   Bacon, my grandmother was a Hogshead of Claret-
wine; my godfathers were these, Peter Pickleherring
and Martin Martlemas[†]-beef; O, but my godmother,
she was a jolly gentlewoman, and well beloved in
every good town and city; her name was Mistress
160   Margery March-beer.[†] Now, Faustus, thou hast heard
all my progeny, wilt thou bid me to supper?

FAUSTUS. No, I'll see thee hanged: thou wilt eat up all my
victuals.[6] *Food*

GLUTTONY. Then the Devil choke thee!

165 FAUSTUS. Choke thyself, glutton! Who art thou—the
sixth?

[5]snacks

[6]food

SLOTH. I am Sloth. I was begotten on a sunny bank, where I
    have lain ever since; and you have done me great injury
    to bring me from thence: let me be carried thither again
170   by Gluttony and Lechery. I'll not speak another word for
    a king's ransom.

[margin: doesn't want to walk]

FAUSTUS. What are you, Mistress Minx, the seventh and
    last?

LECHERY. Who, I, sir? I am one that loves an inch of raw
175   mutton better than an ell of fried stockfish; and the first
    letter of my name begins with L.

[margin: sexual desire]

LUCIFER. Away, to hell, to hell! Now, Faustus, how dost thou
    like this?   [*Exeunt the* Sins.]

FAUSTUS. O, this feeds my soul!

180 LUCIFER. Tut, Faustus, in hell is all manner of delight.

FAUSTUS. O might I see hell, and return again,
    How happy were I then!

[margin: he hasn't seen hell yet]

LUCIFER. Thou shalt; I will send for thee at midnight.
    In meantime take this book; peruse it throughly,
185   And thou shalt turn thyself into what shape thou wilt.

FAUSTUS. Great thanks, mighty Lucifer!
    This will I keep as chary[7] as my life.

LUCIFER. Farewell, Faustus, and think on the Devil.

FAUSTUS. Farewell, great Lucifer.
              [*Exeunt* LUCIFER *and* BELZEBUB.]

190   Come, Mephistophilis.
                       [*Exeunt.*]

[7]careful

CHORUS.

Enter CHORUS.

CHORUS. Learned Faustus,
    To know the secrets of astronomy,
    Graven in the book of Jove's high firmament,
    Did mount himself to scale Olympus' top,
5   Being seated in a chariot burning bright,
    Drawn by the strength of yoky dragons' necks.
    He now is gone to prove cosmography,[1]
    And, as I guess, will first arrive at Rome,
    To see the Pope and manner of his court
10   And take some part of holy Peter's feast,
    That to this day is highly solemnised.

                        [*Exit.*]

[1]features of the universe

SCENE VII.

Enter FAUSTUS *and* MEPHISTOPHILIS.

FAUSTUS. Having now, my good Mephistophilis,
    Passed with delight the stately town of Trier,[†]
    Environed round with airy mountain-tops,
    With walls of flint, and deep entrenched lakes,
5   Not to be won by any conquering prince;
    From Paris next, coasting the realm of France,
    We saw the river Maine fall into Rhine,
    Whose banks are set with groves of fruitful vines;
    Then up to Naples, rich Campania,
10   Whose buildings fair and gorgeous to the eye,
    The streets straight forth, and paved with finest brick,
    Quarter the town in four equivalents:
    There saw we learned Maro's golden tomb,[†]
    The way he cut, an English mile in length,
15   Thorough a rock of stone, in one night's space;
    From thence to Venice, Padua, and the rest,
    In one of which a sumptuous temple stands,
    That threats the stars with her aspiring top.
    Thus hitherto hath Faustus spent his time:
20   But tell me, now, what resting-place is this?
    Hast thou, as erst I did command,
    Conducted me within the walls of Rome?

MEPHIST. Faustus, I have; and because we will not be unpro-
    vided, I have taken up his Holiness' privy-chamber[1] for
25   our use.

FAUSTUS. I hope his Holiness will bid us welcome.

MEPHIST. Tut, 'tis no matter; man, we'll be bold with his
    good cheer.

[1] a private room used exclusively by one person

[handwritten margin note: explaining where M & him have been]

49

And now, my Faustus, that thou may'st perceive
30   What Rome containeth to delight thee with,
Know that this city stands upon seven hills
That underprop the groundwork of the same:
Just through the midst runs flowing Tiber's stream
With winding banks that cut it in two parts:
35   Over the which four stately bridges lean,
That make safe passage to each part of Rome:
Upon the bridge called Ponte Angelo
Erected is a castle passing strong,
Within whose walls such store of ordnance are,
40   And double cannons formed of carved brass,
As match the days within one complete year;
Besides the gates, and high pyramides,
Which Julius Cæsar brought from Africa.

FAUSTUS. Now, by the kingdoms of infernal rule,
45   Of Styx, of Acheron, and the fiery lake
Of ever-burning Phlegethon,[2] I swear
That I do long to see the monuments
And situation of bright-splendent Rome
Come, therefore, let's away.

[2] three of the five rivers the of underworld

50 MEPHIST. Nay, Faustus, stay: I know you'd see the Pope,
And take some part of holy Peter's feast,
Where thou shalt see a troop of bald-pate friars,
Whose *summum bonum*‡ is in belly-cheer.

FAUSTUS. Well, I'm content to compass them some
55   sport,
And by their folly make us merriment.
Then charm me, Mephistophilis, that I
May be invisible, to do what I please
Unseen of any whilst I stay in Rome.
         [Mephistophilis *charms him.*]

60 MEPHIST. So, Faustus, now
Do what thou wilt, thou shalt not be discerned.

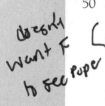

Sound a sonnet.[3] *Enter the* POPE *and the* CARDINAL OF
LORRAIN *to the banquet, with* Friars *attending.*

[3]a set of notes on
the trumpet or
coronet

POPE. My Lord of Lorrain, wilt please you draw near?

FAUSTUS. Fall to, and the Devil choke you an you spare!

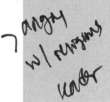

angry w/ religions leader

POPE. How now! Who's that which spake?—Friars, look
65   about.

FIRST FRIAR. Here's nobody, if it like your Holiness.

POPE. My lord, here is a dainty dish was sent me from the
Bishop of Milan.

beating pope cup tsnatching wine/ food from his hand

FAUSTUS. I thank you, sir.   [*Snatches the dish.*]

70 POPE. How now! Who's that which snatched the meat from
me? Will no man look? My lord, this dish was sent me
from the Cardinal of Florence.

FAUSTUS. You say true; I'll ha't.   [*Snatches the dish.*]

POPE. What, again! My lord, I'll drink to your grace.

75 FAUSTUS. I'll pledge your grace.[*Snatches the cup.*]

C. OF LOR. My lord, it may be some ghost newly crept out
of purgatory, come to beg a pardon of your Holiness.

Faustus is in purgatory. Dramatic irony

POPE. It may be so. Friars, prepare a dirge[4] to lay the fury
of this ghost. Once again, my Lord, fall to.
        [*The* POPE *crosses himself.*]

[4]a funeral song

80 FAUSTUS. What, are you crossing of yourself?
    Well, use that trick no more I would advise you.
        [*The* POPE *crosses himself again.*]
    Well, there's the second time. Aware the third,
    I give you fair warning.
    [*The* POPE *crosses himself again, and* FAUSTUS *hits
    him a box of the ear; and they all run away.*]

Come on, Mephistophilis, what shall we do?

85 MEPHIST. Nay, I know not. We shall be cursed with bell,
     book, and candle.

FAUSTUS. How! bell, book, and candle,—candle, book,
     and bell,
     Forward and backward to curse Faustus to hell!

[5]soon

90   Anon[5] you shall hear a hog grunt, a calf bleat, an
     ass bray,
     Because it is Saint Peter's holiday.

cute.

Re-enter the Friars *to sing the Dirge.*

FIRST FRIAR. Come, brethren, let's about our business
     with good devotion.

They sing:

95   Cursed be he that stole away his holiness' meat
       from the table! *Maledicat Dominus!*[‡]
     Cursed be he that struck his holiness a blow on
       the face! *Maledicat Dominus!*
     Cursed be he that took Friar Sandelo a blow on the
100   pate! *Maledicat Dominus!*
     Cursed be he that disturbeth our holy dirge!
       Maledicat Dominus!
     Cursed be he that took away his holiness' wine!
       Maledicat Dominus! Et omnes sancti![‡]
105   *Amen!*

[MEPHISTOPHILIS *and* FAUSTUS *beat the* Friars, *and
fling fireworks among them: and so exeunt.*]

Why fireworks??

CHORUS.

Enter CHORUS.

CHORUS. When Faustus had with pleasure ta'en the view
    Of rarest things, and royal courts of kings,
    He stayed his course, and so returned home;
    Where such as bear his absence but with grief,
5   I mean his friends and near'st companions,
    Did gratulate[1] his safety with kind words,
    And in their conference of what befell,
    Touching his journey through the world and air,
    They put forth questions of Astrology,
10   Which Faustus answered with such learned skill
    As they admired and wondered at his wit.
    Now is his fame spread forth in every land;
    Amongst the rest the Emperor is one,
    Carolus the Fifth, at whose palace now
15   Faustus is feasted 'mongst his noblemen.
    What there he did, in trial of his art,
    I leave untold—your eyes shall see performed.

                            [*Exit.*]

[1] express joy

Robin [handwritten]

SCENE VIII.

Enter ROBIN *the Ostler[1] with a book in his hand.*

Stableman [handwritten]

ROBIN. O, this is admirable! here I ha' stolen one of Doctor
    Faustus' conjuring books, and, i'faith, I mean to search
    some circles for my own use. Now will I make all the
    maidens in our parish dance at my pleasure, stark naked
5   before me; and so by that means I shall see more than e'er
    I felt or saw yet.

Enter RALPH, *calling* ROBIN.

RALPH. Robin, prithee, come away; there's a gentleman tar-
Waits [handwritten] ries[2] to have his horse, and he would have his things
    rubbed and made clean: he keeps such a chafing with my
10   mistress about it; and she has sent me to look thee out;
    prithee, come away.

ROBIN. Keep out, keep out, or else you are blown up; you are
    dismembered, Ralph: keep out, for I am about a roaring
    piece of work.

15 RALPH. Come, what dost thou with that same book? Thou
    can'st not read.

ROBIN. Yes, my master and mistress shall find that I can read,
    he for his forehead, she for her private study; she's born
    to bear with me, or else my art fails.

20 RALPH. Why, Robin, what book is that?

ROBIN. What book! why, the most intolerable book for con-
    juring that e'er was invented by any brimstone devil.

[1] a stableman

[2] waits

55

RALPH. Can'st thou conjure with it?

ROBIN. I can do all these things easily with it; first, I can
25   make thee drunk with ippocras[3] at any tabern[4] in
    Europe for nothing; that's one of my conjuring works.

RALPH. Our Master Parson says that's nothing.

ROBIN. True, Ralph; and more, Ralph, if thou hast any
    mind to Nan Spit, our kitchenmaid, then turn her and
30   wind her to thy own use as often as thou wilt, and at
    midnight.

RALPH. O brave, Robin! shall I have Nan Spit, and to mine
    own use? On that condition I'd feed thy devil with
    horsebread as long as he lives, of free cost.

35 ROBIN. No more, sweet Ralph: let's go and make clean our
    boots, which lie foul upon our hands, and then to our
    conjuring in the Devil's name.

                                             [*Exeunt.*]

Robin + Ralph stole book from
Tavern. The wine maker tells them
to return it. Robin conjures Meph.
Meph gets pissed + threatens to turn
them into an apel dos.

Devil joins F. in Theory.

SCENE IX.

Enter ROBIN *and* RALPH *with a silver goblet.*

ROBIN. Come, Ralph, did not I tell thee we were for ever
made by this Doctor Faustus' book? *ecce, signum.*† here's
a simple purchase[1] for horse-keepers; our horses shall eat
no hay as long as this lasts.

5 RALPH. But, Robin, here comes the vintner.[2]

ROBIN. Hush! I'll gull him supernaturally.

Enter Vintner.

Drawer, I hope all is paid: God be with you;—come, Ralph.

VINTNER. Soft, sir; a word with you. I must yet have a goblet
paid from you, ere you go.

10 ROBIN. I, a goblet, Ralph; I, a goblet!—I scorn you; and you
are but a &c.† I, a goblet! search me.

VINTNER. I mean so, sir, with your favour.
                                        [*Searches him.*]

ROBIN. How say you now?

VINTNER. I must say somewhat to your fellow. You, sir!

15 RALPH. Me, sir! me, sir! search your fill. [Vintner *searches
him.*] Now, sir, you may be ashamed to burden honest
men with a matter of truth.

[1]advantage

[2]wine-maker

57

VINTNER. Well, t'one of you hath this goblet about you.

ROBIN. <u>You lie</u>, drawer, 'tis afore me   [*Aside.*]

20   Sirrah you, I'll teach you to impeach <u>honest men</u>;—
     stand by;—I'll scour you for a goblet!—stand aside
     you had best,I charge you in the name of Belzebub.
     Look to the goblet, Ralph.

                     [*Aside to* RALPH.]

VINTNER. What mean you, sirrah?

25 ROBIN. I'll tell you what I mean. [*Reads from a book.*]
     Sanctobulorum Periphrasticon[‡]—Nay, I'll tickle you,
     vintner. Look to the goblet, Ralph.

                     [*Aside to* RALPH.]

     [*Reads*] *Polypragmos Belseborams framanto*
     pacostiphos tostu,[‡] *Mephistophilis, &c.*

     Enter MEPHISTOPHILIS, *sets squibs*[3] *at their*
     backs and then exit. They run about.

30 VINTNER. *O nomine Domini!*[‡] what meanest thou, Robin?
     thou hast no goblet.

RALPH. *Peccatum peccatorum!*[‡] Here's thy goblet, good
     vintner.

             [*Gives the goblet to* Vintner, *who exit.*]

ROBIN. *Misericordia pro nobis!*[‡] What shall I do? Good
35   Devil, forgive me now, and I'll never rob thy library
     more.

     Re-enter MEPHISTOPHILIS.

MEPHIST. Monarch of Hell, under whose black survey
     Great potentates do kneel with awful fear,
     Upon whose altars thousand souls do lie,
40   How am I vexed with these villains' charms?
     From Constantinople am I hither come
     Only for pleasure of these damned slaves.

[3]sarcastic remarks

ROBIN. How, from Constantinople? You have had a great
    journey: will you take sixpence in your purse to pay for
45   your supper, and begone?

MEPHIST. Well, villains, for your presumption, I transform
    thee into an ape, and thee into a dog; and so begone.
                             [*Exit.*]

ROBIN. How, into an ape; that's brave! I'll have fine sport with
    the boys. I'll get nuts and apples enow.[4]

50 RALPH. And I must be a dog.

ROBIN. I'faith, thy head will never be out of the pottage pot.
                            [*Exeunt.*]

[4]enough

SCENE X.

Enter EMPEROR, FAUSTUS, *and a* Knight, *with* Attendants.

EMPEROR. Master Doctor Faustus, I have heard strange
report of thy knowledge in the black art, how that none
in my empire nor in the whole world can compare with
thee for the rare effects of magic: they say thou hast a
5   familiar spirit, by whom thou canst accomplish what
thou list. This therefore is my request, that thou let me
see some proof of thy skill, that mine eyes may be wit-
nesses to confirm what mine ears have heard reported:
and here I swear to thee by the honour of mine imperial
10   crown, that, whatever thou doest, thou shalt be no ways
prejudiced or endamaged.

KNIGHT. I'faith, he looks much like a conjuror.   [*Aside.*]

FAUSTUS. My gracious sovereign, though I must confess
myself far inferior to the report men have published,
15   and nothing answerable to the honour of your imperial
majesty, yet for that love and duty binds me thereunto,
I am content to do whatsoever your majesty shall command me.

EMPEROR. Then, Doctor Faustus, mark what I shall say.
20   As I was sometime solitary set
Within my closet, sundry thoughts arose
About the honour of mine ancestors,
How they had won by prowess such exploits,
Got such riches, subdued so many kingdoms
25   As we that do succeed, or they that shall
Hereafter possess our throne, shall
(I fear me) ne'er attain to that degree

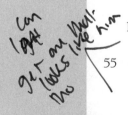

Of high renown and great authority;
Amongst which kings is Alexander the Great,[†]
30   Chief spectacle of the world's pre-eminence,
The bright shining of whose glorious acts
Lightens the world with his reflecting beams,
As when I hear but motion[1] made of him
It grieves my soul I never saw the man.
35   If therefore thou by cunning of thine art
Canst raise this man from hollow vaults below,
Where lies entombed this famous conqueror,
And bring with him his beauteous paramour,
Both in their right shapes, gesture, and attire
40   They used to wear during their time of life,
Thou shalt both satisfy my just desire,
And give me cause to praise thee whilst I live.

[1] mention

FAUSTUS. My gracious lord, I am ready to accomplish
your request so far forth as by art, and power of my
45   Spirit, I am able to perform.

KNIGHT. I'faith that's just nothing at all. [*Aside.*]

FAUSTUS. But, if it like your grace, it is not in my ability
to present before your eyes the true substantial bodies
of those two deceased princes, which long since are
50   consumed to dust.

KNIGHT. Ay, marry, Master Doctor, now there's a sign of
grace in you, when you will confess the truth.
                                    [*Aside.*]

FAUSTUS. But such spirits as can lively resemble Alexander
and his paramour shall appear before your grace, in
55   that manner that they both lived in, in their most
flourishing estate; which I doubt not shall sufficiently
content your imperial majesty.

EMPEROR. Go to, Master Doctor; let me see them
presently.

60   KNIGHT. Do you hear, Master Doctor? You bring Alexander
      and his paramour before the Emperor!

FAUSTUS. How then, sir?

KNIGHT. I'faith, that's as true as Diana turned me to a stag!†

FAUSTUS. No, sir, but when Actaeon died, he left the horns
65   for you.† Mephistophilis, begone.
                          [*Exit* MEPHISTOPHILIS.]

controls
meph

KNIGHT. Nay, an² you go to conjuring, I'll be gone.   [*Exit.*]

²if *conjure the spirit, I'll leave*

FAUSTUS. I'll meet with you anon for interrupting me so.
      Here they are, my gracious lord.

      Re-enter MEPHISTOPHILIS *with* Spirits *in the shape
        of* ALEXANDER *and his* Paramour.

EMPEROR. Master Doctor, I heard this lady while she lived
70   had a wart or mole in her neck: how shall I know whether
      it be so or no?

FAUSTUS. Your highness may boldly go and see.

EMPEROR. Sure these are no spirits, but the true substantial
      bodies of those two deceased princes.
                         [*Exeunt* Spirits.]

75   FAUSTUS. Will't please your highness now to send for the
      knight that was so pleasant with me here of late?

EMPEROR. One of you call him forth!
                         [*Exit* Attendant.]

put horns on his head

      Re-enter the Knight *with a pair of horns on his head.*

      How now, sir knight! why, I had thought thou had'st been
      a bachelor, but now I see thou hast a wife, that not only
80   gives thee horns, but makes thee wear them.† Feel on thy
      head.

[3 cursed]

(handwritten: how dare you give me horns)

(handwritten, cursed)

KNIGHT. Thou damned wretch and execrable[3] dog,
     Bred in the concave of some monstrous rock,
     How darest thou thus abuse a gentleman?
85   Villain, I say, undo what thou hast done!

FAUSTUS. O, not so fast, sir; there's no haste; but, good,
     are you remembered how you crossed me in my con-
     ference with the Emperor? I think I have met with you
     for it.

(handwritten: you crossed me too..)

90 EMPEROR. Good Master Doctor, at my entreaty release
     him: he hath done penance sufficient.

FAUSTUS. My gracious lord, not so much for the injury
     he offered me here in your presence, as to delight you

[4 repaid]

     with some mirth, hath Faustus worthily requited[4] this
95   injurious knight: which being all I desire, I am content
     to release him of his horns: and, sir knight, hereafter
     speak well of scholars. Mephistophilis, transform him
     straight. [MEPHISTOPHILIS *removes the horns.*] Now,
     my good lord, having done my duty, I humbly take my
100   leave.

EMPEROR. Farewell, Master Doctor; yet, ere you go,
     Expect from me a bounteous[5] reward.

[5 generous]

(handwritten: generous)   [*Exeunt.*]

(handwritten: I'll give you an award)

SCENE XI.

Enter FAUSTUS *and* MEPHISTOPHILIS.

FAUSTUS. Now, Mephistophilis, the restless course
    That Time doth run with calm and silent foot,
    Shortening my days and thread of vital life,
    Calls for the payment of my latest years:
5   Therefore, sweet Mephistophilis, let us
    Make haste to Wertenberg.

MEPHIST. What, will you go on horseback or on foot?

FAUSTUS. Nay, till I'm past this fair and pleasant green,
    I'll walk on foot.

Enter a Horse-Courser.[1]

                                               [1]a horse dealer

10 HORSE-COURSER. I have been all this day seeking one
    Master Fustian: mass, see where he is! God save you,
    Master Doctor!

FAUSTUS. What, horse-courser! You are well met.

15 HORSE-COURSER. Do you hear, sir? I have brought you
    forty dollars for your horse.

FAUSTUS. I cannot sell him so: if thou likest him for fifty,
    take him.

HORSE-COURSER. Alas, sir, I have no more!—I pray you
20   speak for me.

MEPHIST. I pray you let him have him: he is an honest fellow, and he has a great charge, neither wife nor child.

FAUSTUS. Well, come, give me your money. [Horse-Courser *gives* FAUSTUS *the money*.] My boy will deliver him to you. But I must tell you one thing before you have him; ride him not into the water at any hand.

25

HORSE-COURSER. Why, sir, will he not drink of all waters?

FAUSTUS. O yes, he will drink of all waters but ride him not into the water: ride him over hedge or ditch, or where thou wilt, but not into the water.

30

HORSE-COURSER. Well, sir.—Now am I made man for ever: I'll not leave my horse for twice forty: if he had but the quality of hey-ding-ding, hey-ding-ding, I'd make a brave living on him: he has a buttock as slick as an eel. [*Aside*.] Well, God b'wi'ye,[2] sir, your boy will deliver him me: but hark you, sir if my horse be sick or ill at ease, if I bring his water to you, you'll tell me what it is.

35

40 FAUSTUS. Away, you villain; what, dost think I am a horse-doctor?   [*Exit* Horse-Courser.]
What art thou, Faustus, but a man condemned to die?
Thy fatal time doth draw to final end;
45   Despair doth drive distrust unto my thoughts:
Confound these passions with a quiet sleep:
Tush, Christ did call the thief upon the cross;[†]
Then rest thee, Faustus, quiet in conceit.
         [*Sleeps in his chair*.]

Re-enter Horse-Courser, *all wet, crying*.

50 HORSE-COURSER. Alas, alas! Doctor Fustian, quotha? mass, Doctor Lopus[†] was never such a doctor: has given me a purgation has purged me of forty dollars;

²God be with you

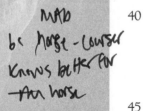

I shall never see them more. But yet, like an ass I was, I
would not be ruled by him, for he bade me I should ride
55 him into no water: now I, thinking my horse had had
some rare quality that he would not have had me known
of, I, like a venturous youth, rid him into the deep pond
at the town's end. I was no sooner in the middle of the
pond, but my horse vanished away, and I sat upon a bottle
60 of hay, never so near drowning in my life. But I'll seek out
my Doctor, and have my forty dollars again, or I'll make it
the dearest horse!—O, yonder is his snipper-snapper.[3]—
Do you hear? you, hey-pass,[4] where's your master?

MEPHIST. Why, sir, what would you? You cannot speak with
65 him.

HORSE-COURSER. But I will speak with him.

MEPHIST. Why, he's fast asleep. Come some other time.

HORSE-COURSER. I'll speak with him now, or I'll break his
glass windows about his ears.

70 MEPHIST. I tell thee he has not slept this eight nights.

HORSE-COURSER. An he have not slept this eight weeks I'll
speak with him.

MEPHIST. See where he is, fast asleep.

HORSE-COURSER. Ay, this is he.—God save you, Master
75 Doctor, Master Doctor, Master Doctor Fustian!—Forty
dollars, forty dollars for a bottle of hay!

MEPHIST. Why, thou seest he hears thee not.

HORSE-COURSER. So ho, ho!—so ho, ho! [*Hollas in his
ear.*] No, will you not wake? I'll make you wake ere I go.
80 [*Pulls FAUSTUS by the leg, and pulls it away.*] Alas, I am
undone! What shall I do?

[3]a small, unimportant person

[4]a juggler

FAUSTUS. O my leg, my leg!—Help, Mephistophilis! call
the officers.—My leg, my leg!

MEPHIST. Come, villain, to the constable.

85   HORSE-COURSER. O lord, sir, let me go, and I'll give you
forty dollars more.

MEPHIST. Where be they?

HORSE-COURSER. I have none about me. come to my
ostry[5] and I'll give them you.

90   MEPHIST. Begone quickly.

[Horse-Courser *runs away.*]

FAUSTUS. What, is he gone? Farewell he! Faustus has his
leg again, and the horse-courser, I take it, a bottle of
hay for his labour. Well, this trick shall cost him forty
dollars more.

Enter WAGNER.

95   How now, Wagner! what's the news with thee?

WAGNER. Sir, the Duke of Vanholt doth earnestly entreat
your company.

100 FAUSTUS. The Duke of Vanholt! an honourable gentleman, to whom I must be no niggard[6] of my cunning.—
Come, Mephistophilis, let's away to him.

[*Exeunt.*]

[5]an Inn

[6]a selfish or
miserly person

SCENE XII.

Enter the DUKE OF VANHOLT, *the* DUCHESS,
FAUSTUS, *and* MEPHISTOPHILIS.

DUKE. Believe me, Master Doctor, this merriment hath much
   pleased me.

FAUSTUS. My gracious lord, I am glad it contents you so
   well.—But it may be, madam, you take no delight in this.
5   I have heard that great-bellied women do long for some
   dainties or other: what is it, madam? tell me, and you
   shall have it.

DUCHESS. Thanks, good Master Doctor; and, for I see your
   courteous intent to pleasure me, I will not hide from you
10   the thing my heart desires; and, were it now summer, as it
   is January and the dead time of the winter, I would desire
   no better meat than a dish of ripe grapes.

FAUSTUS. Alas, madam, that's nothing!—Mephistophilis,
   begone. [*Exit* MEPHISTOPHILIS.] Were it a greater thing
15   than this, so it would content you, you should have it.

   Re-enter MEPHISTOPHILIS *with grapes.*

Here they be, madam; wilt please you taste on them?

DUKE. Believe me, Master Doctor, this makes me wonder
   above the rest, that being in the dead time of winter, and
   in the month of January, how you should come by these
20   grapes.

[handwritten top margin: Winter symbolizes death — end of 24 years]

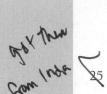

FAUSTUS. If it like your grace, the year is divided into two circles over the whole world, that, when it is here winter with us, in the contrary circle it is summer with them, as in India, Saba, and farther countries in the East; and by means of a swift spirit that I have I had them brought hither, as you see.—How do you like them, madam; be they good?

[handwritten margin: got them from India]

25

DUCHESS. Believe me, Master Doctor, they be the best grapes that e'er I tasted in my life before.

30 FAUSTUS. I am glad they content you so, madam.

[handwritten margin: must reward]

DUKE. Come, madam, let us in, where you must well reward this learned man for the great kindness he hath showed to you.

[1]indebted or grateful

35

DUCHESS. And so I will, my lord; and, whilst I live, rest beholding[1] for this courtesy.

FAUSTUS. I humbly thank your grace.

[handwritten margin: Calls f Master Doctor]

DUKE. Come, Master Doctor, follow us and receive your reward.

           [*Exeunt.*]

SCENE XIII.

Enter WAGNER.

WAGNER. I think my master shortly means to die, *[means F is close to death]*
    For he hath given to me all his goods:
    And yet, methinks, if that death were so near,
    He would not banquet, and carouse and swill
5   Amongst the students, as even now he doth,
    Who are at supper with such belly-cheer
    As Wagner ne'er beheld in all his life.
    See where they come! belike[1] the feast is ended.

[probably]

[*Exit.*]

[1]probably

SCENE XIV.

Enter FAUSTUS *with two or three* Scholars
and MEPHISTOPHILIS.

FIRST SCHOLAR. Master Doctor Faustus, since our conference about fair ladies, which was the beautifullest in all
the world, we have determined with ourselves that Helen
of Greece was the admirablest lady that ever lived: there-
5   fore, Master Doctor, if you will do us that favour, as to let
us see that peerless dame of Greece, whom all the world
admires for majesty, we should think ourselves much
beholding unto you.

FAUSTUS. Gentlemen,
10   For that I know your friendship is unfeigned,
And Faustus' custom is not to deny
The just requests of those that wish him well,
You shall behold that peerless dame of Greece,
No otherways for pomp and majesty
15   Than when Sir Paris crossed the seas with her,
And brought the spoils to rich Dardania.
Be silent, then, for danger is in words.

[*Music sounds, and* HELEN *passeth over the stage.*]

SECOND SCHOLAR. Too simple is my wit to tell her praise,
Whom all the world admires for majesty.

20 THIRD SCHOLAR. No marvel though the angry Greeks
pursued
With ten years' war the rape of such a queen,
Whose heavenly beauty passeth all compare.

73

FIRST SCHOLAR. Since we have seen the pride of Nature's
25   works,
      And only paragon of excellence,
      Let us depart; and for this glorious deed
      Happy and blest be Faustus evermore.

FAUSTUS. Gentlemen, farewell—the same I wish to you.
                           [*Exeunt* Scholars.]

Enter an Old Man.

30   OLD MAN. Ah, Doctor Faustus, that I might prevail
      To guide thy steps unto the way of life,
      By which sweet path thou may'st attain the goal
      That shall conduct thee to celestial rest!
      Break heart, drop blood, and mingle it with tears,
35   Tears falling from repentant heaviness
      Of thy most vile and loathsome filthiness,
      The stench whereof corrupts the inward soul
      With such flagitious[1] crimes of heinous sins
      As no commiseration may expel,
40   But mercy, Faustus, of thy Saviour sweet,
      Whose blood alone must wash away thy guilt.

[1]extremely wicked

FAUSTUS. Where art thou, Faustus? wretch, what hast
      thou done?
      Damned art thou, Faustus, damned; despair and die!
45   Hell calls for right, and with a roaring voice
      Says "Faustus come! thine hour is almost come!"
      And Faustus now will come to do the right.
             [MEPHISTOPHILIS *gives him a dagger*.]

OLD MAN. Ah stay, good Faustus, stay thy desperate
      steps!
50   I see an angel hovers o'er thy head,
      And, with a vial full of precious grace,
      Offers to pour the same into thy soul:
      Then call for mercy, and avoid despair.

FAUSTUS. Ah, my sweet friend, I feel

55   Thy words do comfort my distressed soul.
        Leave me a while to ponder on my sins.

        OLD MAN. I go, sweet Faustus, but with heavy cheer,   [*Exit.*]
        Fearing the ruin of thy hopeless soul.

        FAUSTUS. Accursed Faustus, where is mercy now?
60   I do repent; and yet I do despair;
        Hell strives with grace for conquest in my breast:
        What shall I do to shun the snares of death?

        MEPHIST. Thou traitor, Faustus, I arrest thy soul
        For disobedience to my sovereign lord;
65   Revolt,[2] or I'll in piecemeal tear thy flesh.

        FAUSTUS. Sweet Mephistophilis, entreat thy lord
        To pardon my unjust presumption.
        And with my blood again I will confirm
        My former vow I made to Lucifer.

70 MEPHIST. Do it then quickly, with unfeigned heart,
        Lest greater danger do attend thy drift.
            [FAUSTUS *stabs his arm and writes on a paper with*
            his blood.]

        FAUSTUS. Torment, sweet friend, that base and crooked
            age,[3] old
        That durst[4] dissuade me from thy Lucifer,
75   With greatest torments that our hell affords.

        MEPHIST. His faith is great: I cannot touch his soul,
        But what I may afflict his body with
        I will attempt, which is but little worth.

        FAUSTUS. One thing, good servant, let me crave[5] of thee,
80   To glut the longing of my heart's desire,—
        That I might have unto my paramour
        That heavenly Helen which I saw of late,
        Whose sweet embracings may extinguish clean
        These thoughts that do dissuade me from my vow,
85   And keep mine oath I made to Lucifer.

[2]withdraw from a course of action; retreat

[3]old
[4]dared

[5]beg

MEPHIST. Faustus, this or what else thou shalt desire
Shall be performed in twinkling of an eye.

Re-enter HELEN.

FAUSTUS. Was this the face that launched a thousand ships,
And burnt the topless towers of Ilium?†
Sweet Helen, make me immortal with a kiss.
[*Kisses her.*]
Her lips suck forth my soul; see, where it flies!—
Come, Helen, come, give me my soul again.
Here will I dwell, for Heaven is in these lips,
And all is dross that is not Helena.
I will be Paris, and for love of thee,
Instead of Troy, shall Wertenberg be sacked:
And I will combat with weak Menelaus,
And wear thy colours on my plumed crest:
Yea, I will wound Achilles in the heel,
And then return to Helen for a kiss.
Oh, thou art fairer than the evening air
Clad in the beauty of a thousand stars;
Brighter art thou than flaming Jupiter
When he appeared to hapless Semele:†
More lovely than the monarch of the sky
In wanton Arethusa's† azured arms:
And none but thou shalt be my paramour.
[*Exeunt.*]

SCENE XV.

Enter the Old Man.

OLD MAN. Accursed Faustus, miserable man,
    That from thy soul excludest the grace of Heaven,
    And fly'st the throne of his tribunalseat!

Enter Devils.

    Satan begins to sift me with his pride:
5   As in this furnace God shall try my faith,
    My faith, vile hell, shall triumph over thee.
    Ambitious fiends! see how the heavens smile
    At your repulse, and laugh your state to scorn!
    Hence, hell! for hence I fly unto my God.
        [*Exeunt on one side* Devils—*on the other,* Old Man.]

my Christian faith shall won

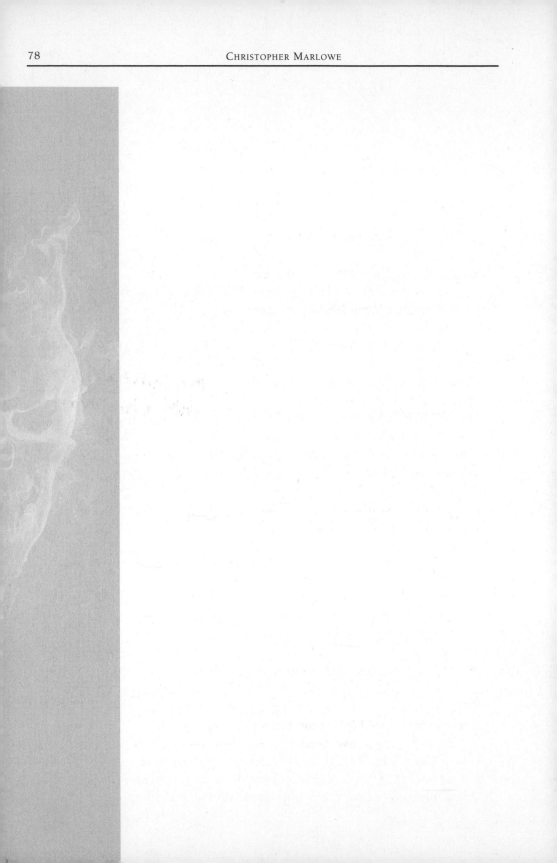

SCENE XVI.

Enter FAUSTUS *with* Scholars.

FAUSTUS. Ah, gentlemen!

FIRST SCHOLAR. What ails Faustus?

FAUSTUS. Ah, my sweet chamber-fellow, had I lived with
thee, then had I lived still! but now I die eternally. Look,
5   comes he not, comes he not?

SECOND SCHOLAR. What means Faustus?

THIRD SCHOLAR. Belike he is grown into some sickness by
being over solitary.

FIRST SCHOLAR. If it be so, we'll have physicians to cure
10   him. 'Tis but a surfeit. Never fear, man.

FAUSTUS. A surfeit of deadly sin that hath damned both
body and soul.

SECOND SCHOLAR. Yet, Faustus, look up to Heaven:
remember God's mercies are infinite.

15 FAUSTUS. But Faustus' offences can never be pardoned: the
serpent that tempted Eve may be saved, but not Faustus.
Ah, gentlemen, hear me with patience, and tremble not
at my speeches! Though my heart pants and quivers to
remember that I have been a student here these thirty
20   years, Oh, would I had never seen Wertenberg, never
read book! and what wonders I have done, all Germany
can witness, yea, all the world: for which Faustus hath

79

lost both Germany and the world, yea, Heaven itself,
Heaven, the seat of God, the throne of the blessed, the
25   kingdom of joy; and must remain in hell for ever, hell,
ah, hell, for ever! Sweet friends! what shall become of
Faustus, being in hell for ever?

THIRD SCHOLAR. Yet, Faustus, call on God.

[margin: Scholars want him to call god]

FAUSTUS. On God, whom Faustus hath abjured! on God,
30   whom Faustus hath blasphemed! Ah, my God, I would
weep, but the Devil draws in my tears. Gush forth
blood instead of tears! yea, life and soul! Oh, he stays
my tongue! I would lift up my hands, but see, they
hold them, they hold them!

[margin: Devil controls him]

35   ALL. Who, Faustus?

FAUSTUS. Lucifer and Mephistophilis. Ah, gentlemen, I
gave them my soul for my cunning!

ALL. God forbid! *[margin: WTF they say]*

FAUSTUS. God forbade it indeed but Faustus hath done
40   it: for vain pleasure of twenty-four years hath Faustus
lost eternal joy and felicity. I writ them a bill with mine
own blood: the date is expired; the time will come, and
he will fetch me.

[margin: Regrets his decision]

FIRST SCHOLAR. Why did not Faustus tell us of this
45   before, that divines might have prayed for thee?

[margin: We would have prayed if we knew you were controlled by devil]

FAUSTUS. Oft have I thought to have done so; but the
Devil threatened to tear me in pieces if I named God;
to fetch both body and soul if I once gave ear to divinity: and now 'tis too late. Gentlemen, away! lest you
50   perish with me. *[margin: WTF I don't want you to die too]*

[margin: was trapped]

SECOND SCHOLAR. O, what shall we do to save
Faustus?

FAUSTUS. Talk not of me, but save yourselves, and depart.

THIRD SCHOLAR. God will strengthen me. I will stay with
55   Faustus.

[handwritten: I'm staying]

FIRST SCHOLAR. Tempt not God, sweet friend; but let us
     into the next room, and there pray for him.

[handwritten: let's go into the other room + pray]

FAUSTUS. Ay, pray for me, pray for me! and what noise soever
     ye hear, come not unto me, for nothing can rescue me.

60   SECOND SCHOLAR. Pray thou, and we will pray that God
     may have mercy upon thee.

FAUSTUS. Gentlemen, farewell: if I live till morning, I'll visit
     you: if not—Faustus is gone to hell.

ALL. Faustus, farewell.
          [*Exeunt* Scholars.—*The clock strikes eleven.*]

65   FAUSTUS. Ah, Faustus,
        Now hast thou but one bare hour to live,
        And then thou must be damned perpetually!
        Stand still, you ever-moving spheres of Heaven,
        That time may cease, and midnight never come;
70   Fair Nature's eye, rise, rise again and make
        Perpetual day; or let this hour be but
        A year, a month, a week, a natural day,
        That Faustus may repent and save his soul!
        O lente, lente, currite noctis equi!‡
75   The stars move still,[1] time runs, the clock will strike,
        The Devil will come, and Faustus must be damned.
        O, I'll leap up to my God! Who pulls me down?
        See, see where Christ's blood streams in the firmament!
        One drop would save my soul—half a drop: ah, my
80   Christ!
        Ah, rend not my heart for naming of my Christ!
        Yet will I call on him: O spare me, Lucifer!
        Where is it now? 'tis gone; and see where God
        Stretcheth out his arm, and bends his ireful[2] brows!

[1]soon

[2]angry, wrathful

[handwritten: freaking out about his last hour to live]

[handwritten: begging for forgiveness]

85   Mountains and hills come, come and fall on me,
And hide me from the heavy wrath of God!
No, no!
Then will I headlong run into the earth;
Earth gape! O no, it will not harbour me!
90   You stars that reigned at my nativity,
Whose influence hath allotted death and hell,
Now draw up Faustus like a foggy mist
Into the entrails of yon labouring clouds,
That when they vomit forth into the air,
95   My limbs may issue from their smoky mouths,
So that my soul may but ascend to Heaven.

                         [*The clock strikes the half hour.*]

Ah, half the hour is past! 'twill all be past anon!
O God!
If thou wilt not have mercy on my soul,
100   Yet for Christ's sake whose blood hath ransomed me,
Impose some end to my incessant pain;
Let Faustus live in hell a thousand years—
A hundred thousand, and—at last—be saved!
O, no end is limited to damned souls!
105   Why wert thou not a creature wanting soul?
Or why is this immortal that thou hast?
Ah, Pythagoras' metempsychosis,† were that true,
This soul should fly from me, and I be changed
Unto some brutish beast! all beasts are happy,
110   For, when they die,
Their souls are soon dissolved in elements;
But mine must live, still to be plagued in hell.
Curst be the parents that engendered me!
No, Faustus: curse thyself: curse Lucifer
115   That hath deprived thee of the joys of heaven.

                         [*The clock strikes twelve.*]

O, it strikes, it strikes! Now, body, turn to air,
Or Lucifer will bear thee quick to hell!

                         [*Thunder and lightning.*]

O soul, be changed into little water-drops,
And fall into the ocean ne'er be found.

                         [*Enter* Devils.]

120   My God, my God, look not so fierce on me!
        Adders and serpents, let me breathe a while!
        Ugly hell, gape not! come not, Lucifer!
        I'll burn my books!—Ah Mephistophilis!

                          [*Exeunt* Devils *with* FAUSTUS.]

I'll burn

black may it

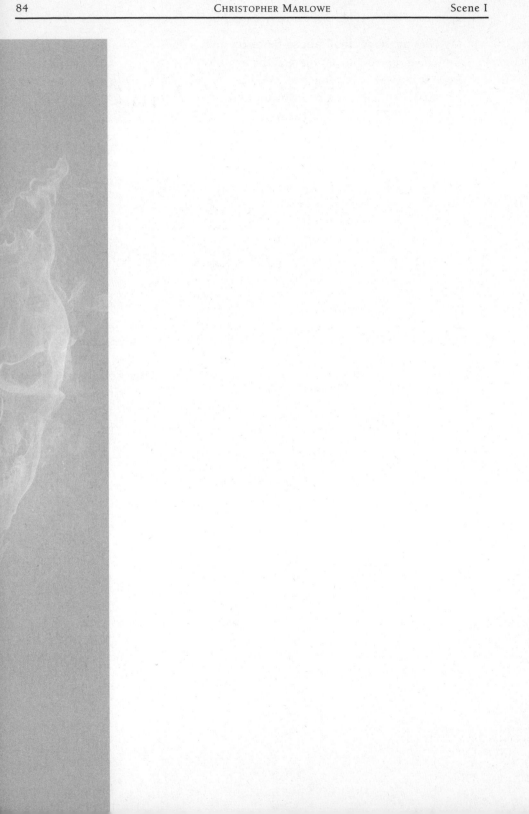

Enter CHORUS.

CHORUS. Cut is the branch that might have grown full
    straight,
    And burned is Apollo's laurel bough,†
    That sometime grew within this learned man.
5   Faustus is gone; regard his hellish fall,
    Whose fiendful fortune may exhort the wise
    Only to wonder at unlawful things,
    Whose deepness doth entice such forward wits
    To practise more than heavenly power permits.

                             [*Exit.*]

Terminat hora diem; terminat auctor opus.‡

The hour ends the day; the author ends the work

          FINIS

Glossary

CHORUS.

Mars – the Roman god of war

Carthaginians – Although the word *mate* means "defeat," in 217 B.C., during the Second Punic War, the Carthaginians (lead by Hannibal) defeated the Romans (lead by Flaminius) at Lake Trasimeno.

waxen wings – Faustus is compared to Icarus. In Greek mythology, Daedalus' son, Icarus, flew too close to the sun, which melted the wings his father had made for him, causing Icarus to fall into the sea.

SCENE I.

Galen – (129-ca.200 A.D.) an important physician in ancient Greece

Justinian – Justinian I (ca.482-565) was the Byzantine Emperor who was famous for the complete revision of Roman law, known as the *Corpus Juris Civilis*, which is the basis for modern day civil law.

Jerome's Bible – called The Vulgate; this is the Latin translation of the Bible by St. Jerome in the 4th century A.D.

German Valdes – possibly Paracelsus (1493-1541), a prominent physician and alchemist

Cornelius – the famous mystic and alchemist, Cornelius Agrippa (63-12 B.C.)

Jove – the Roman god Jupiter, who is the god of the sky and the supreme Roman deity

Prince of Parma – a reference to the "Duke of Parma" (Alexander Farnese 1545-1592), who reestablished Spanish rule in the Netherlands

Antwerp's Bridge – In 1585, during the Eighty Years' War, Farnese's forces built a bridge over the river Scheldt as a blockade during the Siege at Antwerp. It was later blown up by a ship filled with explosives.

Musaeus – a Greek poet and mystic, the pupil or son of Orpheus in Virgil's *Aeneid* VI 667

Indian Moors – refers to Spain's enslavement of American Indians

Lapland giants – an error by the author; the people of Lapland were not known to be giants, but they were said to practice magic.

"…golden fleece…Philip's treasury." – refers to the gold in Prince Philip of Spain's treasury, some of it coming from America; it is also an allusion to the Greek myth of Jason and his search for the mystical golden fleece.

Delphian Oracle – in Greek mythology, the prophetic stone dedicated to Apollo, the god of prophecy

Bacon – Roger Bacon (1214-1294), an English philosopher; his studies are considered by many to be the prelude to modern science.

Albanus – perhaps Pietro d'Albano, a medieval Italian alchemist; perhaps it is a misprint for Albertus Magnus (about 1200-1280).

SCENE II.

phlegmatic – one of the four humors; it was thought that there were four bodily fluids that affected a person's disposition: phlegm, blood, black bile, and yellow bile.

SCENE III.

————

SCENE IV.

————

SCENE V.

Embden – an important commercial town in Elizabethan times

Penelope – In Greek mythology, she was the wife of Odysseus and was faithful to him while he was away for 10 years fighting in the Trojan War.

Saba – the Queen of Sheba

SCENE VI.

Homer – the most acclaimed writer in ancient Greece; the *Iliad* (the tale of the Trojan War) and the *Odyssey* (the travels of Odysseus) are attributed to him. Legend has it that he was blind.

Alexander – another name for Paris, the son of Priam and Hecuba in Greek mythology; his obsession with Helen started the Trojan War.

Oenon – According to mythology, she was a nymph with healing powers and also the first wife of Paris. After Paris left her for Helen, he was wounded during the Trojan War, and he died when Oenon refused to heal him. She then committed suicide.

Thebes – In Greek mythology, Amphion, the son of Zeus and Antiope, built a wall around Thebes by charming the stones.

Martlemas – [*Martinmas*] "the time for drying salted provisions for the winter"

March-beer – Beer brewed in March was the first of the season and very desirable.

CHORUS.

————

SCENE VII.

Trier – also known as Treves, a city in Germany; it was an important commercial city.

Maro's golden tomb – The tomb of Virgil (Maro: 70-19 B.C.) is located in Naples; Maro is the Roman poet who wrote the *Aeneid*.

CHORUS.

————

SCENE VIII.

————

SCENE IX.

&c – This indicates a section that was purposely left blank so the actor could improvise the insult.

SCENE X.

Alexander the Great – (356-323 B.C.) King of Macedonia; the greatest conqueror in the ancient world

"Diana turned to me a stag!"– the Roman and Greek goddess; she turned Actaeon into a stag when he saw her bathing naked.

"...he left the horns for you." – possibly an allusion to the European legend that when a man's wife has been unfaithful, he is made to wear horns in disgrace

"...thou hast a wife...wear them." – See preceding note.

SCENE XI.

thief upon the cross – This is an allusion to Luke 23:32-43 in the Bible, where Jesus assures the thief on the cross beside him that he will have a spot in Paradise, along with Jesus.

Dr. Lopus – Rodrigo Lopez (1525-1594), originally from Portugal, was the personal physician of Queen Elizabeth. Due to prejudice and politics, he was accused of conspiring with Spanish emissaries to poison the queen. He maintained his innocence until his execution in 1594.

SCENE VII.

___

SCENE VIII.

___

SCENE XIV.

Ilium – another name for Troy

Semele – In Greek mythology, she was the mistress of Zeus (Roman: Jupiter). This enraged his wife, Hera, who talked Semele into having Zeus bring forth his lightning bolts. He did so, accidentally killing Semele in the process.

Arethusa – a wood nymph who was turned into a fountain by Artemis to protect her from the god Alpheus, who was pursuing her

SCENE XV.

___

SCENE XVI.

Pythagoras' metempsychosis – a reference to Pythagoras (about 580-490 B.C.), who was a mathematician and philosopher and discovered the geometric theorem that was later named for him; *metempsychosis* deals with reincarnation.

CHORUS.

Apollo's laurel bough – Apollo, the Greek god of the sun, is depicted as wearing a laurel branch around his head.

Latin Glossary

Bene disserere est finis logices – To dispute well is the purpose of logic.

Oncaymaeon – being and no being

Ubi desinit Philosophus, ibi incipit Medicus – Where Philosophy leaves off, there Medicine begins.

Summum bonum medicinae sanitas – The highest aim of medicine is health.

Si una eademque res legatur duobus, alter rem, alter valorem rei, & – If the same thing is willed to two people, one person gets the thing and the other person gets the value of that thing.

Exhaereditare filium non potest pater, nisi, &c. – The father is not able to disinherit the son except when…[This is the typical language of wills; Faustus is putting down lawyers.]

Stipendium peccati mors est. Ha! *Stipendium, &c.* – The wages of sin is death. Ha! Wages, etc.

Si peccasse negamus fallimur et nulla est in nobis veritas – If we claim not to have sinned, we are liars, and there is no truth in us.

Che sera, sera – Whatever will be, will be.

sic probo – this I prove

corpus naturale – natural body

mobile – able to change

Sint mihi dei Acherontis propitii! Valeat numen triplex Jehovoe!
Ignei, aerii, aquatani spiritus, salvete! Orientis princeps
Belzebub, inferni ardentis monarcha, et Demogorgon, propitiamus
vos, ut appareat et surgat Mephistophilis. Quid tu moraris? per
Jehovam, Gehennam, et consecratam aquam quam nunc spargo,
signumque crucis quod nunc facio, et per vota nostra, ipse nunc
surgat nobis dicatus Mephistophilis – May the gods of Acheron (a river in the under-world) look favorably on me! Let the three nods of Jehovah [in classical mythology, if Zeus/Jove nodded three times, it meant that a wish had been granted; here it's Jehovah, the Old Testament God] prevail! Greetings, spirits of fire, air, and water! Beelzebub, Prince of the East, monarch of burning hell, and Demogorgon, we make offering to thee, so that Mephistophilis appears and rises. Why do you delay? By Jehovah, Gehenna, and this holy water which I now sprinkle, and the sign of the cross which I now make, and through our prayers, let Mephistophilis himself now rise up to speak to us.

Quin regis Mephistophilis fratris imagine – Truly you rule in the image of your brother Mephistophilis.

per accidens – by accident

Qui mihi discipulus – One who is my disciple

quasi vestigiis nostris insistere – as if walking in my footsteps

Veni, veni, Mephistophile – Come, come, Mephistophilis

Solamen miseris socios habuisse doloris – It is comforting to the wretched to have had company in their pain (i.e., "misery loves company").

Consummatum est – It is finished.

Homo, fuge – Flee, O man!

situ et tempore – in place and time

intelligentia – intelligence

Per inæqualem motum respectu totius – Because of unequal motion in respect to the whole.

summum bonum – highest good

Maledicat Dominus – God curses

Et omnes sancti – and all that is holy

ecce, signum – behold, a sign!

Sanctobulorum Periphrasticon – Robin is reading from the Doctor's book of magic spells; these are just nonsense Latin words, like abracadabra.

Polypragmos Belseborams framanto pacostiphos tostu, Mephistophilis, &c – nonsense Greek and Latin combined

O nomine Domini – O name of God

Peccatum peccatorum – sin of sins

Misericordia pro nobis – Woe for us (me).

O lente, lente, currite noctis equi – O, run slowly, slowly, horses of the night.

Terminat hora diem; terminat auctor opus – The hour ends the day; the author ends the work.

Vocabulary

CHORUS.

audacious – recklessly bold
conspired – plotted
cunning – skillful; expert
dalliance – recreation; wasting time
divinity – a study of a God-like quality or being
glutted – filled to excess
muse – the source of an artist's inspiration
pomp – a magnificent display
riper – fully mature or advanced
self-conceit – having too high an opinion of oneself
surfeits – overindulges
theology – the study of religion

SCENE I.

ambiguities – unclear or uncertain meanings or intentions
aphorisms – short statements of opinions or truths
argosies – large, cargo-laden merchant ships
artisan – a skilled craftsman
blasphemy – an expression of disrespect for something sacred
canonize – to glorify; treat as sacred; in Catholicism, to be made a saint
canvas – to analyze
concise – short and to the point
conjure – to practice magic to bring forth something
doctrine – a teaching; philosophy, belief
dominion – a territory ruled by one person or entity
enterprise – a difficult or complicated project
illiberal – without culture or refinement
legacies – things that are handed down from the past
maladies – illnesses or unpleasant conditions
mercenary – someone who does something purely for reward or money
necromantic – relating to magic
obscure – unclear; difficult to understand
odious – hateful; detestable
omnipotence – the quality of having unlimited power
ravished – held one's attention; captivated
requisite – necessary for a particular purpose
rudiments – the fundamental elements; basics
scriptures – sacred writings from the Bible
servile – suitable for or like a servant
solitary – secluded

staves – [plural of *staff*] strong sticks used as weapons
syllogisms – statements made from deductive reasoning

SCENE II.

countenance – an expression or composure
lechery – excessive indulgence in sexual activity
licentiates – people who have a degree or license to practice their profession
prone – liable to do something

SCENE III.

abjure – to formally reject
anagrammatized – rearranged letters in words to create other words
confounds – defeats or overthrows
fortitude – the mental strength to endure difficulties
humility – the quality of being modest or meek; lacking false pride
incantations – magical spells
infamous – having a bad reputation
insolence – rudeness
laureate – someone who is worthy of honor for an achievement
pitchy – extremely dark or black
pliant – yielding to others; easily bent
potentate – a ruler or person of great power
proficient – skilled
resolute – firm; determined
voluptuousness – luxury; living life to the fullest

SCENE IV.

familiars – animals or creatures in spirit form that supposedly assist one with magic
plackets – women's ruffled underskirts
vengeance – an act of force or violence
vermin – small, disgusting animals, insects, etc.; or people who are considered as
     such

SCENE V.

bequeath – to give or hand down, especially in a will
chaste – pure; not participating in sexual activity
circumscribed – limited or defined
conditionally – depending on certain terms
congeals – thickens into a mass or clot

contrition – sincere regret for a wrongdoing
courtesans – prostitutes who cater to the upper class
dispositions – personality traits; character
fable – a short story that often uses animals or supernatural beings to teach morals
habitation – a place of residence; home
inscription – a marking, often in the form of writing
inviolate – unbroken; intact
lascivious – driven by lust
perpetual – continuing forever; unending
peruse – to examine in detail
prescribed – established; set down
purified – cleansed of sin; made pure
repentance – regret for past wrongdoing
trifles – things of little importance
vain – silly or foolish
wanton – free-spirited; playful
warrant – to guarantee or attest to

SCENE VI.

aspects – configurations of celestial bodies in relation to each other, thought to influence human affairs
begotten – born of; created or produced
churl – a crude and ill-tempered person of low birth; peasant
conjunctions – the positions of two celestial bodies
covetousness – extreme greed for wealth
disdain – to despise or scorn
empyreal – relating to the sky or heavens
envenomed – made poisonous
famine – a drastic food shortage
firmament – the sky or the heavens
gluttony – excessive eating and drinking
gratify – to reward
henceforth – from this point forward
oppositions – the positions of two celestial bodies that are opposite each other
pension – an allowance; a fixed amount of money given at intervals
progeny – descendants; offspring
rapiers – long, thin, swords used in fencing
renounce – to reject or disown
salvation – saved from the penalty of sin
sloth – an aversion to work; laziness
suffice – to be enough
suppositions – guesses or opinions

CHORUS.

graven – carved or sculpted; a permanent impression
learned – well-educated
solemnized – observed with seriousness

SCENE VII.

discerned – seen or detected
entrenched – firmly established
equivalents – equal parts
perceive – to become aware of through the senses, especially sight or hearing
purgatory – a temporary state or place of suffering one enters after death
stately – impressive in appearance or size
sumptuous – lavish; expensive

CHORUS.

———

SCENE VIII.

brimstone – relating to hell
chafing – irritating or annoying
dismembered – cut or pulled the limbs off
intolerable – impossible to bear

SCENE IX.

drawer – a person who creates an order or bill
gull – to fool or cheat
impeach – to question someone's credibility
presumption – offensively bold behavior
scour – to search thoroughly
survey – to observe carefully
vexed – annoyed; irritated

SCENE X.

bachelor – a single man; a young, low-ranking knight
bounteous – generous; plentiful
concave – curved inward, like the inside of a bowl
endamaged – injured; damaged
entreaty – an urgent plea

injurious – insulting
mirth – amusement; laughter
paramour – a mistress or lover
penance – a punishment; repentance for sin
pre-eminence – the state of being superior
prowess – exceptional skill and/or bravery
renown – widespread honor; fame
subdued – conquered
sundry – various or diverse

SCENE XI.

condemned – sentenced; officially ordered
purgation – a cleansing
venturous – likely to take risks

SCENE XII.

contrary – opposite in direction or position
hither – "to this place"

SCENE XIII.

banquet – to attend a feast
carouse – to drink excessively

SCENE XIV.

afflict – to bring harm or suffering
commiseration – a feeling of pity or sympathy
determined – decided
dissuade – to advise or urge against
drift – the departure from an intended course
dross – waste matter; of little value
extinguish – to bring to an end
heinous – wicked; hateful; deeply criminal
loathsome – causing feelings of disgust
paragon – a model of excellence
peerless – having no equal; beyond comparison
prevail – to succeed
unfeigned – genuine

SCENE XV.

ambitious – eager for success
fiends – devils
repulse – to reject or spurn
tribunal – a court of justice

SCENE XVI.

engendered – produced
entrails – internal parts or organs
felicity – good fortune; happiness
gape – to open wide
harbor – to give shelter
incessant – constant
perish – to die; here, a spiritual death
plagued – tormented
reigned – dominated; ruled
rend – to tear apart violently

CHORUS.
──────